MONSTER

MONSTER

INSIDE THE MIND OF AILEEN WUORNOS

AILEEN WUORNOS
WITH CHRISTOPHER BERRY-DEE

JOHN BLAKE

Dedicated to
Tatiana Dee *nee* Maksina

Published by John Blake Publishing Ltd,
3 Bramber Court, 2 Bramber Road,
London W14 9PB, England

www.blake.co.uk

First published in paperback in 2006

ISBN 1 84454 237 8

British Library Cataloguing-in-Publication Data:

A catalogue record for this book is available from the British Library.

Design by www.envydesign.co.uk

Printed in Great Britain by Bookmarque, Ltd, Croydon, Surrey

3 5 7 9 10 8 6 4

Papers used by John Blake Publishing are natural, recyclable
products made from wood grown in sustainable forests.
The manufacturing processes conform to the environmental
regulations of the country of origin.

Pictures reproduced by kind permission of Rex and Corbis.

CONTENTS

PART THREE
'AND MAY GOD HAVE MERCY ON YOUR CORPSE.'

PART FOUR
MAD OR BAD?

'YOU WANT TO KNOW WHY I KILLED?'

YOU WANT TO KNOW WHY I KILLED? YOU WANT TO KNOW HOW IT HAPPENED? YOU WANT TO KNOW WHY I DID WHAT I DID?

MALLORY WAS THE FIRST. HE WAS A MEAN MOTHERFUCKER. HE ASKED ME IF I WANTED TO SMOKE A JOINT. I TOLD HIM I DIDN'T REALLY SMOKE POT, BUT HE SHOULD DO WHAT HE FELT LIKE DOING – IT DIDN'T BOTHER ME. WE HAD SOME DRINK – I DON'T KNOW WHAT KIND OF LIQUOR IT WAS – AND THEN I ASKED HIM IF HE WANTED TO HELP ME MAKE SOME MONEY. HE WAS INTERESTED, SO WE GO AND WE STOP SOME PLACE OUT ON US I. WE SPENT THE NIGHT DRINKING, AND THEN HE SAID, 'DO YOU WANT TO MAKE YOUR MONEY NOW?'

WE WERE IN THE FRONT SEAT. HE WAS HUGGING AND KISSING ME, THEN HE STARTED PUSHING ME DOWN. 'WAIT A MINUTE,' I TOLD HIM, 'GET COOL.

YOU DON'T HAVE TO GET ROUGH, YOU KNOW. LET'S HAVE FUN.'

'I'VE BEEN WAITING FOR THIS ALL NIGHT LONG.'

'I ALWAYS TAKE MY MONEY FIRST.'

'I WANT TO SEE HOW THE MERCHANDISE FITS.' HE UNZIPS HIS PANTS.

'WELL, WHY DON'T YOU DISROBE OR SOMETHING? WHY DO YOU STILL HAVE TO HAVE YOUR CLOTHES ON?'

'FUCK YOU, BABY. I'M GOING TO SCREW YOU RIGHT HERE AND NOW.'

'NO YOU'RE NOT. YOU'RE NOT GOING TO JUST FUCK ME.'

HE STARTS TO GET VIOLENT. THE SON OF A BITCH. HE'S HOLDING ME DOWN. HE'S GOING TO TRY AND RAPE ME. MY BAG WAS UNZIPPED. I WANTED TO MAKE SURE THAT IF THINGS GOT UGLY I COULD USE MY GUN. HE WAS GOING TO RAPE ME, TAKE MY MONEY, BEAT ME UP, WHATEVER THE HECK HE WAS GOING TO DO.

I JUMPED OUT OF THE CAR WITH MY BAG AND I GRABBED THE GUN. 'GET OUT OF THE CAR!'

'WHAT? WHAT'S GOING ON?'

'YOU SON OF A BITCH, I KNEW YOU WERE GOING TO RAPE ME.'

'NO I WASN'T... NO I WASN'T.'

'YOU KNEW YOU WERE GOING TO TRY AND RAPE ME, MAN.'

'YOU BITCH.'

I SHOT HIM. I SHOT HIM IN THE RIGHT ARM AT FIRST. DIDN'T AIM.

THEN I SHOT HIM ANOTHER THREE OR FOUR TIMES.

HE BEGGED FOR HELP. I DIDN'T KNOW WHAT TO DO. I FIGURED, IF I HELP THIS GUY AND HE LIVES, HE'S GOING TO TELL ON ME AND I'M GOING TO GET IT FOR ATTEMPTED MURDER. SO I THOUGHT THE BEST THING TO DO WAS JUST TO KEEP SHOOTING HIM. AND THEN I THOUGHT, HELL, HE DESERVES TO DIE. HE DESERVES TO DIE FOR WHAT HE TRIED TO DO TO ME. IF I DON'T KILL HIM, HE'LL TRY TO SHOOT ME, AND THEN MAYBE HE'LL GO ON TO TRY AND RAPE SOMEONE ELSE.

I JUST WATCHED HIM DIE.

THE SAME THOUGHTS WENT THROUGH MY HEAD EVERY TIME I KILLED SOMEONE. THE GUY WITH THE .45 I SHOT MORE THAN NINE TIMES. I WAS PISSED OFF WHEN I FOUND THE GUN ON TOP OF THE CAR. 'YOU FUCKING BASTARD,' I TOLD HIM, 'YOU WERE GOING TO BLOW MY BRAINS OUT.' HE CALLED ME A BITCH. HE STARTED GETTING PHYSICAL. I SHOT HIM IN THE BACK SEAT OF THE CAR. I RELOADED THE GUN AND SHOT HIM SOME MORE. THEN I DROVE OVER TO 52 AND DUMPED THE BODY.

I KNOW... I'M PROBABLY LOOKING AT DEATH, BUT I JUST WANT TO GET RIGHT WITH GOD.

I DON'T HAVE A FAMILY, SO I GUESS I DON'T UNDERSTAND THE PAIN I CAUSED THE FAMILY OF THOSE GUYS. WHEN MY STEPMOTHER [ACTUALLY GRANDMOTHER] DIED, MY STEPFATHER WOULDN'T LET ME STAY AT HOME. I WAS LIVING OUT ON THE STREET. I HAD LOTS OF GUYS – MAYBE TEN TO TWELVE A WEEK – AND ON A NORMAL DAY WE WOULD JUST

DO IT BY THE SIDE OF THE ROAD, OR BEHIND A BUILDING OR MAYBE JUST OFF THE ROAD IN THE WOODS IF THEY WANTED IT ALL. I WAS USED TO SEX. THE KIDS AT SCHOOL USED TO FUCK ME, AND SO DID MY OWN BROTHER.

REALLY INSIDE, RIGHT INSIDE ME, I'M A GOOD PERSON. I'VE BEEN WITH LOADS OF MEN – I'VE GONE THROUGH AT LEAST 250,000 GUYS IN MY LIFE, AND I BECAME GOOD FRIENDS WITH SOME OF THEM. THEY REALLY LIKED ME, THEY ALWAYS WANTED TO SEE ME AGAIN. BUT, WHEN JOHNS STARTED MESSING WITH ME, I'D GET JUST AS VIOLENT AS THEY WOULD GET ON ME. I'D LOVE TO SAY THAT TO THEIR FAMILIES. I KNOW THEY MUST THINK I'M A STUPID BITCH, BUT WHAT THEY MUST REALISE IS THAT NO MATTER HOW MUCH THEY LOVED THE PEOPLE THAT DIED, NO MATTER HOW MUCH THEY LOVE THEM, THEY WERE BAD PEOPLE BECAUSE THEY WERE GOING TO HURT ME. SO THEY HAVE TO REALISE THE FACT THAT THIS PERSON, NO MATTER HOW MUCH THEY LOVED THEM OR HOW GOOD THEY FELT THEY WERE, THIS PERSON WAS EITHER GOING TO PHYSICALLY BEAT ME UP, RAPE ME OR KILL ME. I JUST TURNED AROUND AND DID MY FAIR PLAY BEFORE I GOT HURT, SEE? THEY STARTED GETTING RADICAL ON ME, AND I JUST DID WHAT I HAD TO DO...

I WAS BETRAYED ALL MY FUCKING LIFE, YOU KNOW. MY PARENTS BETRAYED ME, MY GRANDPARENTS BETRAYED ME. MEN BETRAYED ME AND THE FUCKING COPS BETRAYED ME. FRIENDS BETRAYED ME. I'VE HAD ENOUGH SHIT IN MY LIFE. WHAT ABOUT THE COPS?

LYING, CHEATING MOTHERFUCKERS. I WAS CLEANING
THE STREETS FOR THEM.

A RAPED WOMAN GETS EXECUTED. YOU ARE ALL
AN INHUMAN BUNCH OF LYING MEN AND BITCHES.
GO AHEAD AND PUT ME IN THE ELECTRIC CHAIR –
YOU'LL ALL GET NUKED IN THE END...

I spend my time trying to get into prisons when most are trying to get out.

I study court transcripts, scene-of-crime photos, witness statements and any document relating to an offender that I can get my hands on. I make it my business to talk with the next of kin, the police, attorneys, schoolteachers and friends. I interview law-enforcement officers, correctional officers, psychiatrists, psychologists and all those who work with these offenders. I talk to the victims' parents and, finally, I get to interview the serial killers or mass murderers themselves.

From the USA to Russia to Singapore, San Quentin to Sablino to Changi, I visit these killers in the human warehouses they call correctional facilities, places where the stench of disinfectant and urine permeates every brick. I touch them and smell the same air they breathe. I sit with them, eat with them. Occasionally I witness their executions.

Collectively, in one space, they are no threat. Just extremely dangerous dead men and women walking, talking – respectful, chatty and cool. Alone with them in their cells – 'houses', in prison parlance – they metamorphose into different beasts; their evil tentacles of thought squirm into your brain. They become controlling, manipulative, sick psycho-beasts. Men such as Kenneth Bianchi and Michael Bruce Ross masturbate every day to the memories of their perverted crimes. I try to communicate and get inside their heads; I try to find out what makes them tick, what makes them do what they do.

My methods occasionally seem to bear fruit. Two homicides (Dzung Tu and Paula Perrera) were cleared up with Michael Ross on Death Row, Connecticut. One murder (Kimberly Logan) was cleared up, amongst other offences, with Arthur John Shawcross, serving 250 years to life in New York.

But I knew there were no crimes to clear up as I drove my rental car down the Dixie Highway to Sheridan Street West to meet Aileen Carol 'Lee' Wuornos at the Broward Correctional Institute, Pembroke Pines, Florida in May 1997. I had just spent time with the Florida Department of Law Enforcement, based in the state capital of Tallahassee, and it was one of those days recently encapsulated by award-winning documentary-maker Nick Broomfield as having '… the promise of sunshine and good times. As the miles unwind, oranges appear on roadside trees and smiles become compulsory as the low-slung sun burns throughout the day.'

Unlike Nick Broomfield, who had spent some time trying to negotiate a visit with Aileen for his acclaimed documentary *The Selling of a Serial Killer*, my opportunity to meet her was offered out of the blue, and I was to talk to a woman whom the media had dubbed the 'Damsel of Death'.

Thankfully I was only with Aileen Carol 'Lee' Wuornos a short while and, to be frank, that limited time in her company was more than enough for me. I guess it was enough for her too. However, I will say this: she was somehow different to any other cold-blooded serial killer, man or woman, I have met, with the exception of Douglas Clark, the Sunset Slayer, who is on Death Row at San Quentin State Prison, California. Both of them were foul-mouthed individuals, and there were certainly no crocodile tears from Aileen Wuornos. As with Doug, there were no mealy, whining, snivelling-laced-with-phoney apologies, no regrets from this brittle woman. Neither of these sociopaths tried the same, well-worn, sympathy-seeking manipulation process so often experienced by psychiatrists, psychologists, investigators and journalists who interview these killers. She looked as hard as granite and, using no fancy sound bites, she spoke her mind – fragmented as it may have been.

What fascinated me above all of the other issues that interested me at the time was not so much why Wuornos had killed – by serial-murderer standards she was small fry with a mere seven, or as I believe eight, victims to her discredit – but why the world's public and media had been whipped into such an all-consuming interest in this particular creature. There are scores of examples of this homicidal breed with higher body counts who are of far more interest in criminological terms, and who might be the focus of similar amounts of mass hysteria. What was the crowd pull for the Aileen Wuornos circus?

Already motion pictures (such as *Monster* and *Overkill*) have been produced which purport to portray the more gruesome segments of her life and crimes. Many TV documentaries concerning Wuornos have been screened around the world. Apart from Jack the Ripper, it is possible that more books have been written about her than any other criminal, or serial killer, who has ever lived. Even police officers, bombarded and tempted by movie consultancy fees totalling $2.5 million, risked their careers in an effort to hike a ride on the Wuornos bandwagon; at least one top cop had to resign.

In life, and even more so in death, Aileen Carol Wuornos has for some reason found herself elevated to cult status. However, no movie has yet dared touch on Wuornos's abused childhood, other than a passing, off-the-cuff reference. Hundreds of ordinary law enforcers were involved with the hunt for Wuornos and Moore, yet they have received no mention for the sterling work they carried out. More importantly, no one has put the spotlight on the glaring inconsistencies in the case. Only one person, as far as I can judge, has been brave enough to name names, and that is Nick Broomfield. I take up the baton from him.

If the story of Aileen Wuornos has any real value at all, it is not entertainment value. It is to expose a criminal justice system for what it was, and probably still is.

Nick Broomfield is not a psychiatrist, as he will confirm, yet he observed that Wuornos was all but insane prior to her execution, and I agree. One does not need to be a shrink to work that one out. Nevertheless, the Florida Department of Corrections stated that she was sane enough to die. My views on capital punishment are just that – my own views. What shrieks out at me is the fact that Wuornos was certainly sane when she committed her horrific murders. She knew the rules. She knew that in committing aggravated murder she might face the ultimate penalty, but she chose to break the rules without a tear of remorse. However, there is not a shred of doubt that her mind disintegrated during her final years. Does this absolve her? Is it some form of mitigation? Too often we consider the killer's human rights – we hear so little of the rights of the victims and the next of kin, their lives wrecked forever.

This book tells Aileen Wuornos's shocking story through her own eyes, and using her own words. These words have been taken from my interviews with her and from the extensive interview tapes taken at the time of her arrest. I have filled in the gaps with my reconstructions of how the events unfolded; I believe them to be as accurate as they can possibly be.

When one sets out to investigate the road to murder, well signposted as it may be, one finds diversions, small, seemingly insignificant dirt roads that can lead to unexpected discoveries. Aileen Carol Wuornos led her eight victims into such diversions where they expected something less than being blasted to death. This book will take you down those roads to a place where you will never look back.

PART ONE

'WHEN I WAS A LITTLE GIRL, I ALWAYS
WANTED TO BE A NUN.'

CHAPTER ONE

THE CIGARETTE
BANDIT

MY MOTHER PLUCKED ME OUT OF HER BELLY AND
LEFT ME WITH MY GRANDPARENTS. WE NEVER KNEW
THE DAMNED WHORE. WE NEVER SAW HER AGAIN
EXCEPT FOR FUNERALS. I SPIT ON HER. SHE CAN GO
TO HELL.

OUR MOTHER SHIT-CANNED US TWO KIDS. THE
MOTHERFUCKING BITCH WHORE SENT US IN A HAND-
BASKET TO HELL.

MY STEPFATHER WOULD BEAT ME OFTEN AFTER
SCHOOL OR IF I CAME HOME LATE. HE'D MAKE ME
CUT DOWN A WILLOW BRANCH AND HE'D USE THAT.
I SOON LEARNED THAT THE THICKER THE BRANCH,
THE LESS IT HURT. SOMETIMES HE USED TO BEAT ME
WITH A BELT, THEN HE MADE ME CLEAN IT.

The twenty-ninth of February is a unique day. It was created artificially to try to make up for the fact that our year is really a few hours longer than 365 days. Aileen Carol Pittman was a Piscean leap-year child. She entered this world, a happy, healthy tot, on Wednesday, 29 February 1956, wrapped up in the warm and secure environment of Clinton Hospital, Detroit, Rochester, Michigan. Her parents were 14-year-old (some say 16-year-old) Diane Wuornos and 19-year-old handyman, sexual pervert and child molester Leo Dale Pittman. Many claim that Leo was a highly sexed, dictatorial figure who carried guns, but we know that they were married with the blessing of his grandmother who lied about their ages. So, one might say, Aileen was born – a dangerous breach birth – with both small feet on the wrong side of the tracks in small-town America.

The marriage between Diane and Leo proved to be tumultuous and, as is all too common in the western world's throwaway society, destined for failure. Indeed, it ended a few months before Lee was born: Leo left the young Diane to raise the new baby and her older brother Keith, a product of the same coupling.

Lee never knew her genetic father, who was soon jailed on the capital charges of kidnapping and raping a seven-year-old girl and taking her across state lines. There is some evidence to suggest that he had also killed a young girl. Leo was to spend some time in two secure mental hospitals. In 1971, while he was in a Michigan prison, this singularly nasty piece of work conveniently fashioned a noose from a bed sheet then hanged himself.

With small-city people living from hand to mouth, it is not surprising that Diane soon found the responsibilities of single motherhood unbearable. Welfare would not help her, and she sought what seemed to her to be the only way out. In 1960, when Lee was four years old, she asked her parents to babysit her kids, then in tears she phoned to say that she would never return.

Lauri Wuornos, a worker in the Ford factory, and his wife, Eileen Britta Wuornos (whom I shall refer to as Britta), already had three youngsters of their own: Barry, Lori and of course Diane, who had become pregnant by the worthless Leo who was now in jail for sex offences. Nevertheless, with the best will in the world, the couple officially adopted both of Diane's children on Friday, 18 March 1960.

Their home, with its sad, yellow-painted wood cladding, was an unprepossessing one-storey ranch amidst a cluster of trees sited off Cadmus Street in Troy, Michigan. Troy sits on Interstate 75 – the Dixie Highway – which features prominently in Lee's life history.

Innocent-looking and otherwise unremarkable, the house, according to Lee, was nevertheless a place of secrets in the rural, close-knit community consisting of dirt roads some 24 miles north of the bustling metropolis of Detroit. Near neighbours, who were never once invited to set foot inside, even for casual pleasantries, recall the curtains always being tightly drawn across the small windows of the Wuornos house. It was common knowledge that Lauri

Wuornos and his wife kept the outside world very much at arm's length. They minded their own business and expected everyone else to attend to theirs.

Aged six, Lee started causing problems at home when she started taking an unhealthy interest in matches. While trying to start a fire with lighter fluid, she suffered scarring facial burns – perhaps a portent for things to come.

Lauri and Britta raised Lee and Keith with their own children, Barry and Lori, but they did not reveal that they were, in fact, the adopted children's grandparents, and, behind those shaded windows, frequent clashes of will took place between young Lee and her heavy-drinking, physically intimidating grandfather. The omnipresent third party was a wide, brown leather belt that he kept hanging on a peg behind his bedroom door. Lee later claimed that, at his bidding, this strap was cleaned almost ritualistically by her with saddle soap and conditioner which were kept in the dresser drawer.

She claimed she was forced to bend, stripped naked, over the kitchen table; the petrified child was beaten frequently with the doubled-over belt. Sometimes she lay face down, spread-eagled naked on her bed to receive her whippings, while all the while her drunken adoptive father screamed that she was worthless and should never have been born. 'You ain't even worthy of the air you breathe,' he shouted, as the belt lashed down again and again.

Sydney Shovan, who grew up two blocks from Lee, rode the same bus to Troy High School on Livernois Road.

Looking back on those days, he recalled with a sigh, 'Lee always had bruises on her arms, cheeks and chin.' He added that everyone knew she was sexually active with her brother Keith. In fact, Keith was teased by the local kids about having sex with Lee while they were both drunk. Lee admits that she was having sex with her brother at an early age – how early we do not know.

'We all used to congregate at a place called The Pits,' said Shovan's sister Cynthia, who was a grade higher than Lee at Troy High. 'One time she was dumped from a moving van, fell badly on her head and no one attended to help her. I guess no one liked her that much.'

In fact, Lee was very much a loner amongst her peers. While the other kids sat around kissing and cuddling, Lee would watch from the fringes. No boys wanted to kiss her, but they *would* buy sexual favours from her in exchange for cigarettes. Thereafter, Lee became known as the Cigarette Pig or the Cigarette Bandit.

During her ninth year, a chemical explosion which Lee and a friend accidentally set off resulted in her sustaining severe burns on her face and arms. She was hospitalised for several days and confined for months afterwards. The burns healed slowly, but Lee worried that she would be deformed and scarred for life. The faint scars on her forehead and her arms bore grim testimony to the accident until the end of her days.

Aged 11, Lee had the shock of her life when she learned that Lauri and Britta were indeed her grandparents. She was already incorrigible, with her fearsome trailer-trash defiance and socially unacceptable temper. But now the girl felt she had been completely deceived. She became uncontrollable and her volcanic verbal explosions, which were unpredictable and seemingly unprovoked, inevitably drove a further wedge between her and her adoptive parents. Her adoptive father, the man she says had so brutalised her as a helpless child, the man who had claimed to be her dad for all those years, was a twisted fraud. She would take out her hatred for him on many of the men she would meet in the future, and she had an excellent tool at her disposal: sex.

Thrashing Lee had never worked – it only served to harden her resolve – so one Christmas her grandfather threw her out into the snow. She lived rough in the woods with a lad for two days before she returned home. Then she was thrown out again and slept in abandoned cars. Following this, and tired of freezing and having nowhere to stay, she ran away for a period of time with a girlfriend called Dawn Botkins. They hitchhiked to California. Dawn would remain Lee's closest friend until the day she was executed.

The two girls would sometimes hitchhike to Hawthorne Park in Detroit, visiting the extremely dangerous Seven Mile Road where they would buy drugs for Lee – she used them all, including downers.

A heavy drinker by the age of 12, on one occasion Lee awoke from a drunken stupor to find dried semen stains all over her clothing. On another occasion, at a party, other children watched as two boys took her while she lay drunk and curled up in the foetal position on the floor. Lee's troubles had well and truly started; soon they would be set in stone.

At school, teachers found Lee to be a poor student with some artistic talent. She could not concentrate, her mind wandered and she seemed to have a convenient hearing problem. By the age of 14, staff were so concerned by her behaviour – in one instance she set fire to a roll of toilet paper in a school washroom – that a teacher wrote, 'It is vital for this girl's welfare that she seeks counselling immediately.' No one took a blind bit of notice, especially her adoptive parents, a lapse which would cost them, eight men and their families dearly.

But she did have one other friend. A man with the Dickensian name of Mr Portlock, he was nicknamed 'Chief'. Hookers would visit him frequently. A creepy guy, Portlock lived in a rundown house close by and he had a reputation as an unsavoury character. Toni Nazar, who was employed as a housekeeper, claimed Portlock was 'a strange, weird man who had cancer'. Lee had no record player at home, so Portlock encouraged her to play her albums at his house while he would sit around leering as she danced. Then, with the young girl on his lap, he would fuss over her and give her money.

Lee became pregnant – some claim it was by her grandfather, or her brother Keith – and was sent to an unmarried mothers' home to await the birth of her child. The staff found her hostile, uncooperative and unable to get along with the other girls in the same boat. Lee gave birth to a baby boy who was put up for adoption in January 1971; the child vanished into obscurity forever.

The stigma of having a pregnant teenage granddaughter proved to be the straw that broke the camel's back. Lauri Wuornos had had enough. He threatened to kill Lee and Keith if they did not leave his house forever. There were terrible arguments between the strict disciplinarian and the more understanding Britta. Then, on 7 July of the same year under somewhat sinister circumstances, Britta Wuornos died. For whatever reason, the man's mind became unhinged. Bizarrely, he attempted suicide by trying to electrocute himself by flooding his basement and standing knee-deep in water with the power on. Shortly afterwards he moved home, and some years later he succeeded in taking his own life. Lauri gassed himself in his garage and Lee stumbled across the body. At his funeral, she turned up only to blow cigarette smoke into the corpse's face.

Diane suspects that her father murdered her mother, although the official story was that she had died of liver failure.

Shortly before her execution, Lee Wuornos radically changed her sentiments about her grandparents; however, by now, as Nick Broomfield confirms, she was tottering on the edge of insanity: 'My dad was so straight and clean... he wouldn't even take his shirt off to mow the lawn. I came from a clean and decent family... my dad blamed me for killing his wife. It was all my fault that she died.'

At her murder trial, Barry Wuornos was called to the witness stand to be questioned by the counsel for the accused, and he faced several searching questions as to Lee's early days. Barry started by stating that, 'It was a normal lifestyle, a pretty straight and narrow family. Very little trouble in the family while Aileen was growing up. They picked her up when I would say she was two years old. Father was a kind of disciplinarian.'

'What was your impression of your father?'

'Well, he was a strong character... a gentle man... laid down strong rules.'

'Did you ever see him beat her? Was he the kind of man who would beat a child.'

'Absolutely not,' came the emphatic answer.

Barry then went on to describe his father's interaction with Lee from the time she arrived at the house until he went into the army.

'Would you describe her grandfather as being abusive?'

'Not at all. Normal spankings, but the general rule was grounding for two or three days.'

'After you left for the service, did you stay in touch with Miss Wuornos?'

'Well, I stayed in contact with my mom and dad.'

'Did your mother and father provide her with a home, shelter, food and clothing?'

'Oh, yes,' came the solid reply.

He began to question the period during which Lee had been badly burned.

'Was medical care denied to Miss Wuornos?'

'She did go to the doctor for a period of eight months and received salves,' Barry replied. 'Mom took care of those things. She was a very quiet, studious, laid-back woman, very in the background. Much easier-going than my father, and no punishment of any kind came from her. My father worked at Ford and Chrysler as an engineer, was a janitor for a while and then worked in quality control ... He was strong on school. He was disappointed because I started at the university and dropped out to go into the service.'

He was not getting the answers he wanted from Barry Wuornos, so he turned up the heat. 'Was Aileen treated differently than any of the rest?' he asked.

'Not that I ever saw,' replied Barry Wuornos. 'One time she was going to be spanked and she brought up the fact that she was adopted and she said, "Don't lay your hands on me. You're not even my real dad." From that time, I never saw any attempts on the part of my dad to physically spank her.'

At the defence table, Lee was visibly angry at her adoptive brother's testimony and she started scribbling furiously on a legal pad.

'When did she learn that she was adopted?' the attorney continued.

'She was ten or eleven at the time. How long before that she knew, I don't know.'

The attorney now turned his focus towards Lee's mother – Barry Wuornos's sister.

'Lee's mother. What was she like?'

'She was like a normal older sister. She had run-ins with her first husband, naturally. We picked up Aileen at the age of two. And she was in no trouble at that point, but before that she was a model student at Troy and she got mixed up with Leo Pittman ... She was with Leo – an on-and-off marriage.'

'What about Aileen's father?'

'I knew very little about Leo. I remember he was trying to date Diane. He was pretty abusive. I remember one day he threw me down and threatened to choke me if I didn't give a message to Diane. He was generally a criminal type ... He was sent to prison and later killed himself.'

The attorney elicited from the witness that Diane had married around the age of 15 or 16 and that it had been a sore point in the family at the time.

'Did Lee do well at school?' asked the lawyer.

'Yeah, I think she did well in school until she reached the ninth grade. She had great artistic ability ... through letters in the service I heard that she was getting into trouble.'

The court learned that Lauri Wuornos drank around a bottle of wine a day, and finally that Barry came home one day and found his father dead in the garage. Lee claims she found her father and her brother was not around.

On hearing the sad news about Lauri, Diane Wuornos invited Lee and Keith to stay with her in Texas, but they declined. Lee, although now a ward of the court, dropped out of school, left home and took up a feral existence, a life of hitchhiking and prostitution, drifting across the country as her spirit moved her.

So, much to the relief of Troy, Lee was leaving on her right thumb. Taking little more than the clothes she wore and carrying a few possessions in a bag, she hit the road, seemingly ill-equipped to start a new life down south. In truth, Lee had all the necessary skills required of the profession that was beckoning. She had good looks, a tough spirit, a neat figure, a cheeky smile, the morals of an alley cat and a strong right hook. She knew what men wanted from her and she would do well out of any gullible guy who crossed her path. Her mind, however, was brooding and silent, a dormant volcano building up to an eruption.

CHAPTER TWO

THE ODD COUPLE

SURE, I THREATENED HIM WITH A MEAT SKEWER. SO
FUCKING WHAT? HE LOOKED AT ME LIKE ALL MEN DID.
RIGHT FROM THE OFF. DIRTY OLD FUCKER.

Lee Wuornos next comes to our attention in 1974 when, using the alias Sandra Kretsch, she was jailed in Jefferson County, Colorado for disorderly conduct, drunk driving and firing a .22-calibre pistol from a moving vehicle. Additional charges were filed when she skipped bail ahead of her trial.

In March 1976, Lee, now aged 20, married multi-millionaire Lewis Gratz Fell. By any measure, this was a curious match. Silver-haired Fell, with his reputable Philadelphia background, was 69 years old when he picked up Lee while she was hitchhiking. He was well connected and kept a plastic business card case containing all of his contacts which included judges, attorneys, state's attorneys and police officers, among others. When Lee and Lewis parted company under somewhat acrimonious circumstances, this wallet went missing, the significance of which we shall soon discover.

Lee saw Fell coming from the word go and, as we now know, this young lady was not one to look a gift horse in the mouth. We have to give her credit for that. However, what we can see is that Lee's first big hit, even if it was not a murderous act, was against an elderly man who was several years older than her grandfather.

Quite what was going through Lewis's mind at that time can only be a matter for conjecture: perhaps he was thinking with the parts he hadn't used for several decades. Nevertheless, he offered Lee his hand in marriage, which she accepted in a heartbeat and, after buying her a *very* expensive engagement ring, they married in Kingsley, Georgia.

The wedding took place less than two months after the death of Lee's 65-year-old grandfather Lauri.

Most of those who knew Lee viewed her marriage cynically. They racked their brains and scratched their heads, finding it impossible to judge it as anything other than a purely mercenary move, which it certainly was. They knew that Lee was capable of just about anything.

The unwitting Lewis Fell had no idea what he was letting himself in for. He was clueless. Some on the fringes took the view that it was a mutually acceptable relationship, and they would be correct. Others thought he was stark raving bonkers. For his part, Lewis had a pretty young woman on his arm and in his bed, while Lee enjoyed the fruits of what his money could buy.

Early in July 1976, husband and wife rolled into Michigan in a brand-new, cream-coloured Cadillac and, while raising a few eyebrows, they checked into a motel. Now smiling all the way to the next bank, Lee stuck a finger up at small-city Troy by sending a few friends newspaper cuttings of their wedding announcement. Carefully clipped from the society pages of the Daytona press, they came complete with a photograph of a man who looked old enough to be her grandfather, knees buckling and leaning heavily on a stick.

Lee knew that word travelled faster over backyard fences than by phone in hick Troy, so, to rub the citizens' noses further in the seed, she highlighted the portion describing Fell as the president of nothing less than a yacht club, with nothing less than a private income derived from nothing less than railroad stocks and shares.

While perky Lee had hit pay dirt, geriatric Lewis had wandered into a very serious problem. His idyllic dream of settling down each night with a young piece of skirt to satisfy his sexual desires was about to become his worst nightmare, one that Stephen King would have been hard-pushed to better.

On Tuesday, 13 July, Lee, against her husband's express wish, decided to go out on the town, while Lewis stayed at home to watch TV. After visiting a few bars she ended up at Bernie's Club in Mancelona where she flaunted her body and started to hustle at the pool table. With a figure many women would die for, clad in an off-the-shoulder top, a micro-miniskirt and thigh-high boots, Lee was as hot as a kitchen stove.

Nevertheless, despite her physical attributes which had the locals drooling at the mouth, sometime after midnight the barman and manager Danny Moore decided he had seen enough of her. Lee was drunk, rowdy, shouting obscenities, uttering threats to other patrons and generally being objectionable. Danny casually walked over to the game and announced that the table was closing down. As he was gathering up the balls, he heard someone shout, 'Duck!' He turned just in time to see Lee aim a cue ball at his head. It missed him only by inches, but the missile had been hurled with such force that it became lodged in the wall.

When a smiling Deputy Jimmie Patrick of the Antrim County Sheriff's Department arrived, Lee was arrested for assault and battery and hauled off to jail. She was also charged on fugitive warrants from the Troy Police Department who had requested that she be picked up on charges of drinking alcohol in a car, unlawful use of a driver's licence and not having a Michigan driver's licence. She was bailed when a friend turned up with her purse containing $1,450 – her husband's money.

Three days later her brother Keith, aged 21, died of throat cancer. It had been in his body for ages and had finally eaten him up. Keith was cremated at the same funeral home as Britta and Lauri Wuornos. Lee arrived late for the service, but in time to place a rose in his hands.

Having rejected her son in life, but acknowledging him in death, Diane flew in from Texas for Keith's funeral. Other mourners were surprised to see her apparently too distraught to sit through the service for the son she had abandoned.

The reader does not need to be a clairvoyant to predict that things did not bode well between Lee and Lewis, and that the marriage would be short-lived. Lee had been torn between her desire to get drunk and hang out in bars, and the less desirable option: long periods of abject boredom, sitting around at her aged husband's feet in his plush, beachside condominium, their eyes glued to TV programmes about trains, boats and the stock market. With problems looming from every direction, Lewis tried the well-tested and universally approved 'I am older than you, please respect your elders' trick. Trained most comprehensively in this area by her late adoptive father, whose family communication skills were considerably less than poor, Lee responded by awarding her new husband a black eye.

Shaken, and very likely stirred, by this outburst from his sweet young wife, Lewis tried another idea. After all, it had worked with his late wife, and the other two before that, so why shouldn't it work with his new one? He would cut Lee's allowance, and, if that failed, he would not give her any money at all. After considering the plan overnight, breakfast came. Dressed in his gown, his feet warm in his furry slippers, he got as far as saying, 'I will stop your allow–' when she beat him up with his walking cane and pointed a meat skewer uncomfortably close to his throat.

Lewis Fell now saw the light. At the first opportunity he obtained a restraining order to prevent another battering, and sought an annulment of the marriage claiming she had squandered his money and given him several damned good thrashings into the bargain.

The divorce decree stated:

Respondent has a violent and ungovernable temper and has threatened to do bodily harm to the Petitioner and from her past actions will injure Petitioner and his property ... unless the court enjoins and restrains said Respondent from assaulting ... or interfering with Petitioner or his property.

Lee pawned the expensive diamond engagement ring he had given her. Lewis Fell, his bank account seriously depleted, vanished into obscurity a wiser man. Their marriage officially ended on Tuesday, 19 July 1977 with a divorce issued at the Volusia County courthouse in Florida.

On Thursday, 4 August 1976, Lee pleaded guilty to the assault-and-battery charge, paying a fine and costs of $105. Then came an unexpected windfall. Keith's army life insurance paid up and, as next of kin, Lee received $10,000. The money was immediately put down as a deposit on a shiny black Pontiac (which was soon repossessed). She also bought a mixed bag of antiques and a massive stereo system, although she had no home in which to put them. Lee blew all the money within three months.

Adrift in the world once again, Lee embarked on a series of relationships which, as may have been expected, failed. From time to time she turned tricks, but, even as a prostitute working the interstate highway, she was not exactly sought after.

For a while in 1981, she lived in a mobile home with a retired businessman who was separated from his wife. 'Lee was quick-tempered,' he said, but he found her 'warm, loving and resourceful'. She did all that she could to please him, and he recalled that, when the vacuum cleaner broke down, she replaced it with a new one the very same night – albeit stolen it from a nearby hotel.

Lee was deeply in love with him, but one night they quarrelled and Lee awoke in the morning still angry, feeling that this man might be just like all the others who had taken advantage of her over the years. On Wednesday, 20 May, she took the car, bought a six-pack of beer, then stopped at a pawn shop to buy a pistol and some bullets. She drove for hours, despondent and contemplating suicide, but, instead of turning the gun on herself, she held up the Majik Market in Edgewater, Florida, while dressed in shorts and a bikini top.

'I was fed up with living,' she said. 'I had no car, no money, no family. I had nothing. Struggling seemed senseless. I even tried to join the service – the army, navy, air force – but you needed 42 points to pass, and I always missed by exactly five points. So I was going to kill myself.

'I drank a case of beer and a quarter pint of whiskey. I also took four reds. Librium. I got my boyfriend's car and went to this store. I grabbed a six-pack of beer and two Slim Jims. I had $118 on me.

'I walked up to the counter and put my purse on it. The handle of my gun was sticking out, and the woman started screaming like hell about how I was going to rob the store. She freaked out, and I said, "What the hell, you want a robbery, then I'll rob your store. Give me your money."'

The clerk handed her $33 from the cash register.

'I walked out of the store real slowly, because I was so drunk and I couldn't find my keys. I sat in the car for three minutes looking for them. Then I drove away and started hauling ass down the highway. Then the radiator blew and I had to stop, and these kids helped me push it to a gas station. I was wearing one of those country hats, and I took that off, and the shorts, so I was just in my bikini. I was trying to alter my description and that's when the fucking cops arrived.'

She would later add, 'In order to test his love for me, I held up a convenience store. If he loved me, he would have gotten me out of that fix. I didn't give a fuck.'

Russell Armstrong was the criminal defence attorney who represented Lee on the charges of armed robbery in 1981. He found 25-year-old Lee bright but suicidal, and asked the judge, Kim C. Hammond, to order a psychiatric evaluation prior to trial. Dr George W. Barnard examined Lee and arrived at the following conclusion:

The prisoner is a 25-year-old white divorced female who has an appreciation of the charges against her and she says she does not know the range and nature of the possible penalties. She understands the adversary nature of the legal process and has capacity to disclose to attorney pertinent facts surrounding the alleged offense, to relate to attorney, to assist attorney in planning her defense, to realistically challenge prosecution witnesses, to manifest appropriate courtroom behavior, to testify relevantly, to cope with the stress of incarceration prior to trial and is motivated to help herself in the legal process. It is my medical opinion the defendant is competent to stand trial, was legally sane at the time of the alleged crime and does not meet the criteria for involuntary hospitalization.

Lee was sent to the Florida Correctional Center in Lowell on Thursday, 4 May 1982 where she was disciplined six times for fighting and disobeying orders. Released on Thursday, 30 June 1983, she went to live with middle-aged Thomas Sheldon, one of several prison pen pals. Tom immediately realised that she had problems. He tried to get psychiatric help for her, but the clinic he contacted refused to admit her for treatment when she claimed, quite wrongly, that her problems were all his fault. After a few months he sent her back to Florida. Her previous boyfriend would not take her back. Rejection was following Lee like a ghost, haunting her every relationship.

In January 1984, Lee drifted into New Smyrna Beach, just south of Daytona Beach, where she moved in with a retired truck driver for a few months. 'Two men came and dropped her off one day,' he would later tell reporters. 'She needed a quiet place to stay. She cleaned and cooked. I wanted somebody quiet, because it's a quiet neighbourhood. She seemed bitter somehow, but she always put herself together. She could have taken advantage of me if she had wanted. She did have a temper, but was a pretty girl.'

On Tuesday, 1 May 1984, Lee was arrested for attempting to pass a forged cheque at the Barnett Bank in Key West, Florida. She had foolishly forged her employer's signature on two cheques – one for $5,000 and the other for $595. She was bailed, and two years later she pleaded guilty to forgery after the prosecution agreed to drop related charges. Sentencing was set for 30 April 1986. She did not show up and a warrant was issued for her arrest.

On Saturday, 30 November 1985, she was named as a suspect in the theft of a pistol and ammunition in Pasco County. The victim was a man who had given her a few nights' board and lodgings in return for sex. During this year she had her first recorded lesbian affair with an Italian woman called Toni in Florida Keys. The relationship was passionate, enlivened by frequent jealousies and physical violence. Toni and Lee had travelled to Orlando and purchased equipment to start a steam-cleaning firm, and Lee said that it was her own earnings that had paid for it.

'Toni, she was like a really good friend,' Lee recalled. 'I wasn't alone any more. I wanted to stay with her.'

After several months, Lee says she came home to find Toni, the cleaning equipment and all of her possessions gone. 'The only items left behind,' she said, 'were a fan and a phone bill for $485. She was using me. I was so upset about losing a business that I'd have had for the rest of my life.'

Shortly after this bust-up, Lee borrowed the alias of Lori Grody from an aunt in Michigan and, 11 days later, the Florida Highway Patrol cited Grody for driving with a suspended licence. On Saturday, 4 January 1986, her rap sheet shows she was arrested in Miami under her own name and charged with auto theft, resisting arrest and obstruction by giving false information. Police found a .30-calibre revolver and a box of ammunition in the stolen car. She was bailed and vanished.

On Monday, 2 June 1986, Volusia County deputies questioned Lee after a male companion accused her of pulling a gun on him and demanding $200. In spite of her denials, Lee was carrying spare ammunition in her pockets and a .22-calibre pistol was found underneath the passenger seat she had occupied. She was charged with grand theft and carrying a concealed firearm. Again she failed to appear in court and another bench warrant became outstanding.

A week later, using the new alias of Susan Blahovec, she was ticketed for speeding in Jefferson County, Florida. The citation included a telling observation: 'Attitude poor. She thinks she is above the law.'

Later that year she was arrested in Dade County for grand larceny and resisting arrest. Eventually the charges were dropped.

At this point in the life of Lee Wuornos, it is perhaps of value to take a brief look back and refresh our minds. Lee has said that she suffered an abusive childhood, contradicting the evidence given in court by her adoptive brother Barry. Indeed, Lee would apportion all of the blame for her failings, and later crimes, on the way she was raised by her grandparents, only then to say, when she was on the verge of insanity, that she came from a clean and decent family.

After leaving home, there is no doubt that Lee was exploited by men; but she also used men, and her own words prove that she had no real concerns or morals about this. However, what does shine through is her need to be wanted and loved.

Throughout the many years during which I have studied the psychopathic personality, I have noted in more cases than I can even recall that these offenders blame their antisocial behaviour for the most part on the alleged treatment meted out to them by others. More often than not these criminals are simply not mentally equipped to shoulder the blame for their crimes themselves. And Lee seems to be cast in the same mould. It was always others who failed her, but there is never a mention from Lee of her perhaps failing herself: it was her genetic mother and father; her adoptive parents; the alleged systematic abuse she suffered at their hands, and at the hands of her peers. She claimed Lewis Fell was at fault, as were several of her on-and-off-again boyfriends who failed to understand her needs, who were unable to make her happy and secure. She blamed Toni for stealing the cleaning equipment and her own belongings – all matters where Lee is the innocent, wide-eyed party. Surely we can see a pattern developing.

We know that by this time in Lee's turbulent life she had a criminal record that included armed robbery – a trivial amount of money was stolen, but armed robbery is still a serious offence. She was a forger and a hooker who could be an honest, hardworking girl one moment, a spitting demon the next. Lee carried firearms and she was prepared to threaten people with them. She thought she was above the law.

When Lee met 24-year-old Tyria 'Ty' Jolene Moore at a Daytona gay bar in 1986, she was lonely, angry and ready for something new.

CHAPTER THREE

TYRIA JOLENE MOORE

IT WAS LOVE BEYOND THE IMAGINABLE. EARTHLY
WORDS CANNOT DESCRIBE HOW I FELT ABOUT TYRIA.
I THOUGHT TYRIA MUST BE TAKEN CARE OF AS SHE,
HERSELF, HAD NEVER BEEN. THE ONLY REASON I
HUSTLED SO HARD ALL THOSE YEARS WAS TO
SUPPORT HER. I DID WHAT I HAD TO DO TO PAY THE
BILLS, BECAUSE I DIDN'T HAVE ANOTHER CHOICE. I
HAD WARRANTS OUT FOR MY ARREST. I LOVED HER
TOO MUCH. THEN THE FUCKING BITCH SOLD ME
DOWN THE RIVER. I HATE THE BITCH.

Wearing the oldest non-American Indian place name in
the United States, Florida, or 'Place of Flowers', was so
dubbed by the Spanish explorer Juan Ponce de Leon when
he became the first known European to set foot on what
would eventually become US soil, on 2 April 1513. By all

accounts Juan found much gold in the rivers of the 'Island of Florida' and, in doing so, upset a few of the natives. In July 1521 he was mortally wounded by an Indian arrow and returned to Havana, Cuba, where he gracefully expired.

We owe modern Florida, especially its seaside resorts, to one of the greatest go-getters of his age. Carl Graham Fisher was a wealthy magnate who designed and built most of America's major highways. In the late 1910s, Fisher became seized with the idea that Miami Beach – or Lincoln, as he wished to call it – would make a splendid resort.

The costs and logistics of building a resort in a distant swamp proved formidable, but Fisher persevered and by 1926 had nearly finished his model community, complete with hotels, a casino, golf courses, a yacht basin and a lavish Roman swimming pavilion (which featured, a trifle incongruously, a Dutch windmill).

Then a hurricane blew it all down.

As if this was not enough, when the stock market crashed in 1929, the market for holiday homes disappeared. Fisher would not live to see the success that Miami Beach became.

Covering 55,560 square miles, Florida is now famous for its beaches which stretch along the entire eastern seaboard from Fernandina Beach in the north to Miami in the south. The Sunshine State has the air of being one large, glitzy holiday resort, with glamorous hotels lining its long coastline. But behind the style lies a seamier side. It is this same coast that has brought drug smugglers to the state. It is a favourite retirement area – its balmy climate appeals to the elderly – but it also attracts a large vagrant population who find the weather suits their pockets: sleeping outdoors is free. Florida is not only a tourist state, but also home to a large transient population. These wanderers pick up seasonal work on fruit farms where they are badly paid, or they fall in with the local drug trade. Many of them are women, so Lee, often dressed in black leather, was not conspicuous as a lone female hitching on her own.

Getting to Daytona Beach was easy for Lee. She had run away from home and run away from her marriage. She had crossed state line after state line with the law on her tail, hitched south on Interstate 95 and found what she thought was paradise: sunshine, jobs and cheap living.

According to those who knew Lee and middle-class, respectable Tyria, it had been love at first sight in June of 1986 when the two met at the now-defunct Zodiac Bar in South Daytona. Lee was still on the run after passing forged cheques; it is reported that Tyria had received an insurance payout resulting from a car accident and was well away from her home town of Cadiz, Ohio. She was working as a laundry maid at the El Caribe Motel at 2125 Atlantic Avenue and living on Halifax Drive with her friend, Cammie Greene, who had taken her in after she was evicted from her apartment.

Mr and Mrs Greene were good people. They were law-abiding, Sunday-barbeque folk who always went out of their way to help their neighbours, baked cakes and were well liked. 'Tyria and we were good friends,' Mrs Greene told reporters, 'at least until we met Aileen. My husband and I finally asked them to leave because we didn't want their lifestyle in our house.'

Lee had not only told Tyria that she had a steam-cleaning business, but also had told the same untruth to the Greenes. She would go off to 'work' carrying a briefcase. One day, Lee arrived home with a black eye, claiming she had been raped by a stranger for six hours. This made Cammie Greene suspicious. While the girls were out, she opened the briefcase and discovered it was full of condoms and men's business cards. She tried to warn Tyria but the truth was Tyria already knew that Lee was a hooker, and she found it exciting.

On the day she left, and as repayment for the Greenes' hospitality, Lee stole Cammie's identification, including her driver's licence: Cammie was about to become one of the aliases used by the emerging monster.

To keep Tyria's love and companionship, Lee ploughed more and more hours into prostitution. She invested time in Tyria who was a born-again Baptist with close ties to the Calvary Baptist Church where she had been recently baptised. Tyria had attended Bible-study lessons and sometimes babysat for the Reverend David Laughner who had become her friend as well as her minister. Tyria met with limited success in sharing her religious beliefs with Lee who knew the Bible and could recite scripture, but whose actions were so often in conflict with Tyria's more traditional background, even more so with the Bible itself.

Tyria became born-again in 1984, just two years before the two women met, but this lady from a God-fearing family had her own conflicts with scripture. She was now living in a lesbian relationship.

For a while, Lee and Tyria lived together at the El Caribe Motel. But money was scarce, and in the spring of 1987 Tyria approached a friend she had known from church and asked if she could rent a room on the understanding that Lee and Tyria slept in separate beds. The scriptures, the woman said sternly, explicitly forbade homosexual/ lesbian relationships. 'The Lord,' she recited, 'wants you to be with a man. That's why they're here.'

Lee had had her fill of Bible-thumping and of men. She flipped. 'Don't try to force me to be with a man,' she hissed. 'I was married to a man and he beat me! I can't even talk about my father! That's why I am this way – because of men!' This outburst was something of a reversal of the truth. Lee had only been married once, to the luckless Fell, and she had beaten him, not vice versa.

Regretfully, the friend asked the two to leave her home at once. She liked Tyria, whom she recalled as being 'all sweet, all smiles, real soft', and wished she could help her. 'I'm not holding Lee responsible for what happened to her,' she confided to Tyria before they parted company, adding in a hushed tone, 'but I think you should tell her to go her own way.'

For a while life was great. Tyria loved Lee and stayed close to her. Lee called Tyria her 'wife'. Uncannily Tyria, with her strawberry-red hair, freckled face and stocky build, eerily resembled Leo Pittman, the father Lee never met. Tyria claims she quit her job as a motel maid for a while, which meant that Lee supported her with earnings from prostitution.

At first, this departure from regular employment was no major financial setback because Tyria only earned $150 a week while Lee could, if she worked hard enough, earn that much in a day. In due course, though, their ardour cooled and money began to run short. Still Tyria stayed with Lee, following her like a puppy from cheap motel to cheap motel, with stints in old barns, or in the woods, in between.

In March 1987, Tyria and Lee bought an old Corsair trailer. How they funded this purchase is a mystery: Lee said she financed it, but she earned a pittance from prostitution so Tyria's account seems to be the honest one where she claims she borrowed the money from a friend. Their first and only stop in the trailer was the east-coast Ocean Village Camper Resort in Ormond-by-the-Sea, but once again their stay was short-lived. They had a constant stream of hippies and down-and-outs calling upon them, and they littered their surroundings with junk. Wearing little more than underwear on occasions, and exploiting their toughness, the two women became the talk of the park.

Billy and Cindy Copeland rented the space for the women's trailer and lived next to them. Billy later somewhat dramatically said, 'Lee had some cruel eyes –

death-row eyes, I call them. I don't know what that means
– that's just the way they make you feel. I know that girl
could kill you in a heartbeat, but I always liked her.'

Things came to a head at the Ocean Village Camper
Resort during the early hours of one morning when a
volley of shots echoed around the site and the neighbours
were subjected to very loud country-rock music
emanating from Lee and Tyria's trailer. They were ordered
to leave immediately.

They returned to Daytona where, on Friday, 18
December 1987, a highway-patrol officer cited Lee, who
was using the alias Susan Blahovec, for walking on the
interstate and possessing a suspended driving licence.
The citation noted 'Attitude poor', and 'Susan' proved it
over the next few months by sending threatening letters
to the circuit-court clerk on 11 January and 9 February
1988. As for what happened to the trailer, no one seems
to know.

On the occasions when Lee could not hitch a ride, she
would catch a bus. The anger of this woman was
apparently well known among bus drivers who picked her
up. Terry Adams, operations supervisor of Voltran, the
Volusia Country Transit company, was 'swamped' with
reports from his drivers that Lee was 'nasty mostly and
threatening them with bodily harm, cursing at them
because of certain situations'.

On Saturday, 12 March 1988, using the alias of Cammie
Marsh Greene, she accused Daytona bus driver Richard

Loomis of assault, claiming that he had pushed her off a bus following an argument. Tyria Moore was listed as a witness to the incident which concerned the confrontation with the black bus driver, who said, 'She started screaming and hollering, "I'm not going to tell you where I am going or my name or where I live or anything." If she had her way, she would sit down and just ignore everybody. If for whatever reason she got on and started, which was frequent, it would be like she was trying to find a way to argue with you ... she always mentioned men. I don't know of a woman driver in the place that ever had trouble with her.'

Richard Loomis recalled that his bus picked Lee and Tyria up near I-4 and 92 and he commented to Tyria that she was 'looking good'. 'Well, Aileen didn't care for this,' Loomis told the court at Lee's trial. 'She punched me right in the mouth, and I knocked her through the door, I think.'

Driver Metcalf was another victim of Lee's abusive behaviour. 'Well,' he said, 'when she was at the bus stop, say when you pull up and the buses have kneelers on them. And she would say, "Kneel the fucking bus, you asshole" or "You nigger, you cocksucker" ... She was just mean as a rattlesnake.'

On Saturday, 23 July 1988, Daytona landlord Alzada Sherman accused Tyria Moore and 'Susan Blahovec' of vandalising their apartment, ripping out carpets and painting over the walls in dark-brown paint without her approval. At this time, Tyria was back working as a maid at the Casa del Mar Motel, 621 South Atlantic Drive, Ormond

Beach. Alzada Sherman, Tyria's friend at the motel, was later questioned by both defence and prosecution counsel about that period. Once again, we can gain a valuable insight into the turbulent domestic affairs of this lesbian couple, and more importantly into the mind of Lee, who was now a troublesome, loud-mouthed, hard-drinking hooker.

'Now, you indicated before you went on record that Lee and Tyria stayed with you for a month?'

'Uh-huh.'

'And that is the address you gave at the beginning?'

'Exactly.'

'Did you live at the motel that you were working in?'

'No.'

'What was the name of the motel?'

'Casa del Mar.'

'But they stayed at your apartment?'

'Yes. I have a two-bedroom apartment.'

'They shared one of the bedrooms?'

'One of the bedrooms. It wasn't supposed to be that way.'

'How was it supposed to be?'

'It was told to me that Lee was going away for a year and a half and she wouldn't be back. And Tyria needed a place to live. I liked Tyria. So I needed a roommate at the time to share the rent. So I offered her the room. To share the rent.'

'Did she initially move in by herself?'

'Yes.'

'How long was it before Lee moved in there?'

'Well, Ty moved in on the Friday. Lee moved in on the

Sunday. She left and I thought she was gone, but she showed up again on the Wednesday.'

'Was there any conversation between Friday and Sunday about her possibly moving in?'

'No.'

'What happened on that Sunday?'

'I confronted Tyria about it. And she said, let her spend the night and she'll be gone in the morning, which she was. But then she shows back up Wednesday. It was like every other day she would come back.'

'And did that routine go on throughout the month?'

'Yes. And I told them they had to move.'

'What would be said to you, typically, each time she would come back to spend the night?'

'She had no place to go.'

'And did you ever ask them where she was during those days that she wasn't there?'

'Yes. Their answer was "working".'

'Did she say where she was working?'

'Lee said she was working in Orlando. She did floors with those big machines.'

'Pressure-cleaning-type things?'

'Yes.'

'So, she would be gone for a day or two and show back up?'

'Then she showed back up. Sometimes she would come at night in a cab.'

'During that time frame when Lee would come back in, would she ever have anything with her that she didn't have when she left?'

'No. She always took a bag, like a – when you go to the gym, you know, gym bags. That's the kind of bags she would leave with. And she would come back with the same bag.'

'While Lee was in your home, how did she act?'

'Very difficult. When she wasn't drinking, she was calm. But when she drank, she was loud and obnoxious.'

'How often would she be drinking?'

'During the time she stayed there that's all she did, mostly.'

Alzada told the court that Busch and Budweiser seemed to be Lee's favourite drinks, and that her drinking sessions were often followed by loud arguments with Tyria behind the closed bedroom door.

'Can you estimate, when she was there drinking, how much she might drink in an evening or a day?'

'Normally she would come in with a 12-pack and maybe drink two or three 12-packs in a night and in a day. She is a heavy drinker. They trashed the place.'

Lee often said she liked sex with men, and her sex life with Tyria waned enough for Tyria to complain to her best friend about it. Lee herself said that her 'greater love' for Tyria 'wasn't sexual'. The real driving force in Lee's life wasn't sex at all; it was a search for an emotional bond and love – love that she had never really had from her abandoning mother, her emotionally and physically abusive grandfather or, it seems, from the grandmother who failed to protect her from him, and certainly not from the callous young males who had sex with her while she was an adolescent. She was far more familiar with loss than with love, having lost her brother Keith to cancer, and having had her baby son snatched from her after she gave birth. Lee found the deep emotional bond she desperately craved with Tyria. Her borderline personality disorder carried with it an overwhelming fear of abandonment. She would do anything to keep her, even kill if needs be, and so deep-seated was her love for Tyria, she would even give up her life to protect her in the years to follow.

Lee's market value as a hooker, never spectacular, fell even further. When Lee hit the road searching for johns, she would pose as a hitchhiker or a disabled motorist at highway on-and-off ramps – she became an 'exit-to-exit prostitute'. Money was always tight and they were constantly moving from lodgings to lodgings because they failed to pay the rent. Their existence, meagre though it was, became more difficult to maintain. Clearly something had to change, but getting out of Daytona was not easy. There was never enough money to get to Miami, and the two women now realised that jobs were scarcer than they had first thought. They had blown all their money, and their dreams of good times had faded as quickly. Desperation crept in, and temptation was quick to follow. It is a formula that often leads to crime. In November 1988, Lee was causing problems once again. Using the alias Susan Blahovec, she launched a six-day campaign of threatening phone calls against a Zephyrhills supermarket following an altercation over lottery tickets.

Sometime during the Christmas of 1989 and New Year 1990 – the dates and details are sketchy at best – James Dalla Rosa picked up Lee who showed him a photo of two children and said that she was a high-class call girl who lived in a $125,000 home. She pulled from her bag a plastic case with various business cards – formerly the property of Lewis Gratz Fell. 'These are some of my customers,' she told James, who felt very uncomfortable with the situation and didn't feel that everything was as advertised. Lee quoted $100 for sex in a motel, $75 for sex in the woods and $30 for oral in the car – rates that she was to keep until she was arrested. Sensing that the man had money, she said, 'I prefer to go into the woods,' Dalla Rosa later testified.

When he spurned her offer, she became agitated, 'moving jerkily, bouncing in her seat, snatching at her purse', as the driver described her behaviour. 'She became angry after I was not receptive to her offer. Her demeanour changed tremendously.'

He dropped her off near an interstate where she slammed the door and stormed off.

PART TWO:

'OF COURSE I DIDN'T REALLY WANT
TO KILL THEM IN MY HEART, BUT I
KNEW I HAD TO.'

CHAPTER FOUR

RICHARD MALLORY

Murdered 1 December 1989

THE TRICKS? MAN, HOOKERS ARE THE SAME AS CAB DRIVERS. YOU GET GOOD FARES AND BAD FARES. SOME GUYS ARE OK AND GIVE RESPECT. OTHERS TREAT YOU LIKE SHIT. SOMETIMES YOU GET PAID, OFTEN THE JOHNS COMPLAIN. STRAIGHT HO'S STRIP, ROUND THE WORLD, MAYBE A BLOWJOB. I AIN'T NEVER BEEN A SOCIAL WORKER. DON'T GIVE GREEN STAMPS. THEY WANT TO FUCK... THEY PAY, OK? THEY FUCK UP MY HEAD, RAIN ON MY PARADE, THEY GOT WHAT COME TO THEM. MALLORY? HE WANTED TO CUFF ME AND RAPE ME, YOU KNOW. THAT'S WHAT DID IT FOR ME.

THAT CANCER-RIDDEN FUCKING JUDGE SAID I KILLED HIM FOR MONEY. HEY! I HAVE BEEN WITH HUNDREDS OF MEN WHO HAD MONEY. I ONLY KILLED SEVEN, SO WHAT DOES THAT TELL YOU? AND THAT'S

45

THE FUCKING TRUTH. THE COPS KNEW I KILLED MALLORY. I LEFT MY PRINTS EVERYWHERE. THEY JUST COVERED IT UP. HEY, I JUST WANT TO GET IT OVER WITH. NO TEARS. TOUGH IT OUT AS MUCH AS I CAN. JUST LAY ON THAT TABLE, SMILE, AND GET OUT OF HERE.

IT WAS HIS CHOICE. KILLING MALLORY WAS NOTHING TO ME. I WAS COLD AND WET. JUST TRYING TO HITCH A RIDE AND THIS GUY GOES PAST, STOPS AND COMES BACK. HE WAS OK AT FIRST... HE HAD A BOTTLE OF VODKA THEN WE STOPPED FOR BEERS AT A GAS STATION, HE GOT DORITOS AND STUFF. SURE, HE JUST CHATTED. HE WAS RUNNING LATE BECAUSE OF THE TRAFFIC AND THEN WE TALKED ABOUT SEX. THAT'S ALL THEY FUCKING WANT.

I DON'T RECALL THE TIME, MAYBE AROUND 3AM. WE CROSSED A RIVER TOWARDS DAYTONA BEACH. HE PULLED OFF THE ROAD, UP A TRACK AND INTO WOODS. WE WERE IN THE FRONT SEATS. I STRIPPED AND WE DRANK MORE BEER, SMOKED AND KISSED FOR A WHILE. JUST STUFF. HE WAS LIMP AND HE GOT PISSED WITH ME. HE HIT ME. WANTED TO FUCK ME WITH HIS LIMP DICK. I GAVE HIM A BLOWJOB AND THEN HE WENT FUCKING CRAZY. LIKE A CRAZY MAN. SLAPPED ME SOME AND HELD ME DOWN, AND FUCK YOU, MAN, NO MOTHERFUCKER DOES THAT TO ME. HE WAS GOING TO RAPE ME. I AM TELLING YOU, LIKE I TOLD THE JUDGE, HE WAS RAPING ME...

WHAT I'M SAYING... YOU WANT THE TRUTH? I

WANT TO TELL IT AS IT WAS. I'M TELLING YOU THAT
I WAS ALWAYS GOING SOMEWHERE, AND MOST TIMES
I HITCHED A RIDE. THERE ARE THOUSANDS OF GUYS
AND WOMEN OUT THERE WHO'LL SAY THEY GAVE ME
A RIDE, AND WE GOT ON JUST FINE, YOU KNOW. THEY
GAVE ME NO HASSLE. I'M A GOOD PERSON INSIDE, BUT
WHEN I GET DRUNK, I JUST DON'T KNOW. IT JUST...
WHEN I'M DRUNK IT'S, DON'T MESS THE FUCK WITH
ME. YOU KNOW? THAT'S THE TRUTH. I'VE GOT
NOTHING TO LOSE. THAT'S THE TRUTH.

I WAS ALWAYS SHORT OF MONEY, SO I GUESS
SOMETIMES I BROUGHT UP SEX. MALLORY WANTED
TO FUCK STRAIGHT OFF. HE WAS A MEAN
MOTHERFUCKER WITH A DIRTY MOUTH. HE GOT
DRUNK AND IT WAS A PHYSICAL SITUATION, SO I
POPPED HIM AND WATCHED THE MAN DIE. SPEARS
WAS MADE OUT TO BE A NICE, DECENT GUY. THAT'S
SHIT. HE WANTED A QUICK FUCK. HE BOUGHT A FEW
BEERS AND WANTED A FREE FUCK... AND YOU WANT
TO KNOW ABOUT THE THIRD ONE? HOW DO YOU
THINK HE GOT UNDRESSED? WISE UP. HE WANTED
SEX... GOT UNDRESSED. ASK YOURSELF, WHAT'S THAT
ALL ABOUT IF HE DIDN'T WANT A CHEAP FUCK? THE
COPS DIDN'T SAY ABOUT THE OTHERS... NEVER
FOUND THE JOHNNIES. YEAH, OK, MAN. LOOK, YOU
GOT TO UNDERSTAND THAT GUYS DON'T GET NUDE
WITH SOME BROAD IF THEY DON'T WANT SEX. THE
LAST ONE... I CAN'T REMEMBER WHAT HIS NAME
WAS... JESUS CHRIST... HE WAS FUCKING ENGAGED.

HE BOUGHT A SIX-PACK. THE DIRTY MOTHERFUCKER.

AND I DO HAVE ONE THING, THOUGH, THEIR FAMILIES MUST KNOW, THAT NO MATTER HOW THEY LOVED THE PEOPLE THAT I KILLED, THEY WERE BAD BECAUSE THEY WERE GOING TO HURT ME. I SUPPOSE YOU THINK I REALLY SUCK, RIGHT?

I JUST SHOT MALLORY IN HIS RIGHT ARM. DIDN'T AIM. NOTHING. JUST SHOT HIM MAYBE THREE OR FOUR TIMES RIGHT THERE. HE BEGGED FOR HELP, BUT I WATCHED HIM DIE... SURE I ROBBED HIM... SO WHAT?

I will cut straight to the chase here. As Lee would suggest, 'Cut the fucking crap.' The police knew it, many potential witnesses knew it and the prosecutor knew it. The judge refused to admit it at trial, and the jury lived in sublime ignorance of the fact that Richard Charles Mallory was a sexual deviant.

'He didn't attempt to rape you,' roared the judge. 'You brutally shot Mr Mallory for his money.'

Lee's sentiments: 'Fuck you. I hope you, your wife and fucking kids die of cancer.'

The jury at Lee's trial had no way of knowing this, but there is no doubting that Richard Charles Mallory liked to put himself about. The 51-year-old owner of a Clearwater electronics-repair business used to close up shop abruptly and disappear for a few days at a time on binges of heavy drinking and perverted sex. It was his secret life.

With no male friends, he was an extremely secretive,

paranoid loner. It has been claimed that Mallory changed the locks to his apartment many times in the three years before his death. It is also said that he had been involved with an ambassador's wife; he certainly appeared paranoid whenever this woman was mentioned. He thought he was being followed and wanted to have plastic surgery to get his nose altered, presumably so he wouldn't be recognised. He was a strange fellow indeed, this Richard Mallory.

He employed staff only long enough to clear the backlog of work that accrued during his disappearances, and let his workers go once his repair orders were up to date. Perhaps this was a prudent, financially astute move for a man whose credit cards were no longer valid, a man who needed every dime for something far more appealing...

Unbeknown to the jury, the only constants in Mallory's life – apart from his unexplained absences from work – were heavy alcohol consumption and an insatiable desire for sex. He used the services of hookers, visited strip joints and was seriously into hardcore pornography. He also used drugs. Apart from a recent girlfriend, no one – including the jury at Lee's trial – was aware that he had served the better part of ten years in the Maryland State Mental Institution for an attempted rape.

Mallory was a private man, and an enigma to everybody. Living alone in a multi-family apartment complex called The Oaks, few people came to know him on account of his erratic lifestyle; at his television- and video-repair shop, Mallory Electronics in Palm Harbour, his absences were frequent and unexplained.

With a population of just under 60,000, one might have thought that Mallory's business would have done a roaring trade in the Clearwater area. He knew his stuff, turned out quality repairs and didn't charge his customers a fortune. However, he had squandered all of his firm's profits on deviant sex. He was in serious financial straits. Bankruptcy loomed over Richard Mallory and his company. To kick off with, he owed serious money. The sums included $4,000 in rent arrears for the business, and a small packet on his apartment. The credit card companies had closed his accounts. Business transactions were now all in cash. He was due to be swept up, closed down and evicted by his landlords. His business affairs were due to be audited by the Inland Revenue Service. He had stalled the inspectors for too long, and pressure was mounting. The result was that Mallory had a good many problems on his mind.

Some would say he was a good-looking man with his full head of dark hair combed back from a high forehead. Standing at just less than six feet tall, the neatly moustachioed Mallory surveyed the world through hazel eyes behind wire-rimmed glasses. He cut a trim figure, tipping the scales at just less than 170 pounds, and he thought of himself as 51 years young. Five times divorced and recently separated from an entirely decent girlfriend called Jackie Davis, Mallory had always been drawn to the opposite sex and seedy exchanges. He loved to party in the debauched sense, and was a regular visitor to the kinds of adult-entertainment establishments dedicated to catering to pleasures of the flesh.

Mallory liked the way women looked, the way they smelled and moved. He liked the way he felt when he was with them – powerful, controlling, sensuous. He liked power over women; he liked to abuse them, to tie them up, handcuff them, bite them and knock them around. To him, street women and those who flaunted their bodies were up for ill treatment.

When Richard Mallory didn't show up to open his shop on Monday, 3 December 1989, his staff and clients didn't think much of it. As far as friends went, there was no one close enough to him to notice he was gone. Frankly, no one even cared. It wasn't until the cops turned up at his business saying they had found his abandoned Cadillac outside Daytona that anyone knew anything was amiss. No one 'gave a rat's ass', as one officer dryly observed.

'The best beach in Florida! A perfect destination for honeymooners and couples! Vacation values that won't bust your budget!' So scream the tourist brochures. But Daytona is no different to many cities: along the star-spangled sidewalks, lined with laundromats, strip joints and seedy hotels, Joe Public can get his 'round the world' (everything) for 80 bucks, or a straight 'ho's strip' (where the hooker strips for oral only) for 20. Richard was a sufficiently regular customer at the topless bars in the Tampa, Clearwater and Daytona areas that the strippers, go-go dancers and hookers mostly knew him by sight, if not by name. When he latched on to them, he was like a rigged fruit machine – guaranteed to pay out nearly every time.

The weather had closed in on Thursday, 30 November 1989. Rolling in from the Gulf of Mexico, the storm front had been snapping its leaden skies at Florida's east coast for several hours. To the west, the palms from Cape Coral all the way north to Cedar Key were whistling; the rain, at first a heavy spatter, now became a thundering torrent. Flash floods were probable and gale warnings had sent sensible folk scurrying home.

Out on Interstate 4, Richard Mallory was cursing his bad luck – as if he didn't have enough problems without his light-beige, two-door Cadillac Coupé de Ville with tinted windows being wedged in traffic. It would have been a long haul at the best of times. He had had a good run out of Pinellas County across Old Tampa Bay on I-275 along the glistening Howard Frankland Bridge, but now he was stuck like a belligerent cork in a bottleneck. Making Orlando would take him ages now, and on top of that it would be another 60 minutes before he hit Daytona Beach where his fun could start.

Above him, a Med Air chopper was fighting its way through the rain to a railroad trestle where a hobo had jumped the metals and been hit by a train. He has lost both legs: it's terminal. Looking down from the chopper, the observer takes in the interstate, pumping from the heart of Tampa like a knotted artery twisting and turning 30 miles east to Brandon and on to Orlando in the grey distance. Just outside the city limits, the traffic has congealed into a solid mass as hundreds of vehicles, their tail lights glowing red, slither to a standstill along the highway.

Down there, on the eastbound lane, the observer sees the red and blue flashing strobes of light bars. Highway Patrol officers have lit flares and are busy with the wreck of an overturned truck. That's what's causing the snarl-up. The chopper banks sharply and clatters away into the night.

Among this traffic congestion, Mallory lights a reefer, takes another slug of Smirnoff vodka and taps his fingers impatiently on the wheel, cursing again and again...

The traffic edged forward at a snail's pace, and his patience was now threadbare. He had closed up shop early, rushed home to change into jeans and a pullover, thrown a few things into a bag, then headed east for Daytona and a long weekend of drinking and pleasure. Mallory had chosen not to drive either of his white or maroon company vans: if he wanted a quick lay, the Cadillac, with its plush brown interior and tinted windows, was far better suited to the pursuit of pleasure.

Mallory's mind was full of urgency now. Earlier in the week he had confided in a customer, somewhat boastfully, that he hated being around Clearwater with the people gossiping behind his back. The truth is that his criminal record meant it was a place where he had to keep his nose clean. He was always pushing his luck, but on his home patch he had to treat the hookers and bargirls right. They were all whores but, although Mallory had kept out of serious trouble for years, if he slipped up he would be back behind bars before he could blink. Out of town, away from Tampa, he could do more or less as he wished. He could use and abuse women. He could, if the mood took him, treat them like shit.

Suddenly the long tail of red brake lights in front of him switched off. His time for brooding was over. He took another draw on his reefer and, with his windscreen wipers slapping back and forth, he pushed the car into gear and was on the move.

Now the rain was coming down in sheets. There was a slight wind, and the rush of heavy traffic was whipping the water up into a spray. He had driven a short distance when suddenly a figure thumbing for a lift appeared in his headlights. Mallory slowed down and took a sly look. It was a woman, aged around 30, of medium build and carelessly dressed in cut-off jeans, T-shirt and baseball cap. His pulse raced and he sucked in his breath. He felt the need of company – if it was a woman, so much the better. After stopping the car, he hooked his right arm over the back of the passenger seat, looked through the rear window and reversed to where she stood.

Fate keeps a close hand. There is a point along the road to a murder where things are set in motion: one life ends, the other is irrevocably changed. In this instance, a few minutes either way and the paths of victim and killer would not have crossed. Had Mary Christiansen missed the skidding truck, even by a millisecond, she would now be at home, fit and well. The road accident that caused the traffic jam that night would not have happened, and Mallory would have been long gone on his way to Florida's east coast. The domino effect, however, had started: the first one had tipped over near Tampa; the last one would fall along a dark, remote track in Volusia County near Daytona Beach.

If only he had not noticed Lee. Any one of a hundred or so drivers could have stopped for this lonely woman; indeed, many had already given her a ride that day and lived to tell the tale. After her arrest, for those men it would be a memory they would never forget. In their nightmares they would recall the hitchhiker chatting in their cars. Maybe they had sensed all was not good with her. Her manic little laugh; her hints at sex. But they had lived; Richard Mallory, on the other hand, had a rendezvous with death.

Bisexual Lee, who had never killed a man in her life, had been drinking way down in Fort Myers. For a few nights she hustled for money, then she had an argument with Tyria over the phone. She had been on the road since 6am and her mood, right now, was not good. However, she had the better part of $250 in her purse to put down as a deposit on a new rented apartment in Burleigh Avenue. Now, after six rides north, she was about to climb into a car with a sexual predator.

Lee was happy with the chance of a ride and drawled that if he was on his way to Daytona that was just fine. As they moved off, Mallory asked her if she minded him smoking the reefer. She laughed and told him he could do what he liked, but she didn't touch drugs herself. She did, however, accept his offer of a drink. He always kept booze in his car, so they began to get friendly and drunk.

'I thought he was kind of funny. Don't often take a ride and have a joint pushed your way,' Lee said to me. 'To start with, the fucker was kind of cute.'

With shifty sidelong glances at his passenger, Mallory, who was not averse to paying for sex, almost immediately weighed her up as a hooker who had hit hard times. She had a mottled complexion, straggly blonde hair, thin, somewhat cruel lips, a cute nose, great legs and the wet T-shirt accentuated her firm breasts. She had a manly way about her and was a tad on the heavily built side, but the more he knocked back the booze, the better she looked.

Although a little abrasive, Lee was a chatty, forthright lass, so he was not surprised when she asked him if he would like to 'have some fun and help her make some money'. Mallory replied saying he might be interested. Lee would later confirm that this was her usual modus operandi. She always brought up the issue of sex, and several witnesses who had given her rides would testify to this.

Mallory told her he knew girls in topless bars and bragged he would pay $2,000 per photo session. He talked about politics, religion and that his electronics store was going through troubled times. Just past Orlando he stopped for petrol. He bought a six-pack of beer and went to the bathroom. Upon returning to the car he talked about his ex-wife and having problems with a lady. Lee could identify with his troubles and, at that moment, murder was the furthest thing from her mind. All she needed to do was get back to Tyria, pay the deposit on the new apartment, shift their personal belongings and move in.

We have no reason to doubt Lee when she claims that they turned into a stopping point just off US Highway 1 and continued to drink and talk until nearly 5am. The place was too wide open for sex, so they drove on towards Daytona and Mallory asked the woman who gave her name as Lee if she wanted to make her money now.

'My rates were easy to understand, even for a drunk,' she explained to me. 'Head for $30; $35 straight; $40 for 50/50 [half oral/half vaginal penetration]; $100 an hour.' According to Lee, she agreed to $30. Evidence at autopsy that Mallory may have only opened his zip, yet had his pants belted at the waist, testifies to Lee's claim that he just wanted a $30 blowjob.

They swung off Interstate 95 and drove up a track which she knew as the Quail Run, which ended in deserted woodland. Leaving the headlights ablaze and switching on the interior light, Mallory and Lee swung open their car doors. Shortly after her arrest she stated that Mallory gave her the money she wanted and she began to strip off her few clothes. Usually she would ask the men to strip too, and certainly to remove their pants. Mallory didn't.

At first, she said she provided him with the service he required then he attacked her. At trial, she changed the story by saying that he had refused to pay her anything, tied her up, beat her and forced a blunt object into her anus. She was sure he was going to kill her, so she broke free and shot him. 'It was just another trick,' she told me during our interview. 'It was cool and royal before it went sour.'

When she was naked, she asked him if he wasn't going to do the same. But it seems that Mallory had no intention of undressing. Merely unzipping his trousers, he rolled drunkenly on top of the woman, smothering her face in kisses. Even through his alcoholic haze, Mallory would have seen that a sudden change had come over her. One minute she had been just another good-time girl hoping to make a fast buck. Now she looked like an avenging fury, her face a distorted mask of hatred. 'You son of a bitch,' she hissed. 'You were going to rape me.'

She said they began to hurl abuse at each other, Lee repeatedly accusing Mallory of attempted rape. Ignoring her, he rolled on top again, this time more forcefully. But Lee succeeded in wriggling away from him and out of the car, taking her shoulder bag with her. We will never know the exact truth of the sordid scenario, but something happened in that car which sparked a monstrous fury in Lee – she had never been so enraged before in her life. She had been with scores of johns; countless men had paid her for sex, yet, up until that moment in time, Lee had not shot anyone. Why was Richard Mallory so different?

When Mallory looked up, it was to see her standing naked with a small-calibre pistol aimed straight at him.

'What's going on?'

'Get out of the car,' Lee ordered.

He hesitated before starting to sidle over to the passenger seat. When he was in the doorway, she backed away. He made to lunge at her but she squeezed the trigger of the .22-calibre, nine-shot pistol. The gun jumped in her hand, the sharp crack of the report shattering the stillness of the early-morning air. Mallory moaned as the round struck him in the upper part of his left arm, passed clean through it and lodged in his rib cage. Bewildered, he managed to stand up outside the car. Lee backed still further away from him, holding the weapon in a police grip for deadly accuracy. She pulled off two more rounds in quick succession. He was now mortally wounded.

The copper-covered, hollow-nose bullets tore into the right and left of Mallory's chest. As he jerked under the impact of the third shot, the frenzied Lee let off a series of rounds, one of which struck Mallory in the side of the neck above the collarbone. He fell to the ground. Both of his lungs had collapsed; blood was pouring into his body. He wheezed in a futile fight for air.

Meanwhile, his killer coolly got dressed and chose what she liked among his belongings, then squatted down on her haunches and watched. After just over ten minutes, Mallory's wheezing stopped.

The next day, Mallory's Cadillac was found suspiciously abandoned near John Anderson Drive in Ormond Beach, a short distance from where Lee and Tyria were staying. Deputy John Bonnevier and County Deputy Sheriff John Bondi were out on routine patrol when they stopped to examine the vehicle parked up in a sunny clearing. Two doors were open, the interior light was on. Peering inside, they noticed what appeared to be bloodstains behind the steering wheel, but there were no signs of either the driver or, for that matter, any passengers. John Bondi would later testify at trial: 'On 1 December 1989, in the course of routine patrol, at or about 3.20pm, I discovered an abandoned vehicle in a wooded area on John Anderson Drive … I conducted an enquiry around the vehicle looking for a driver … failed to find anyone in the area.'

Officer Bondi added that the vehicle's ignition keys were not in the switch, but numerous items were found a short distance from the car. Partially buried in the sandy soil was a blue nylon wallet containing Richard Mallory's Florida driving licence, miscellaneous papers and two long-expired credit cards. There were also two plastic tumbler glasses, a half-empty bottle of Smirnoff vodka, an empty bottle of Budweiser and a red car caddy, along with several other items, all of which suggested that Mallory had not been alone. An examination of the driver's seat revealed that it had been pulled as far forward as it would go, into a driving position which would have been extremely uncomfortable for a man of Mallory's size. There was a trail of items leading down the track to the main road.

Further examination of the vehicle revealed a pair of prescription spectacles under the front seat and, in the boot, the impression left by a toolbox which had apparently been removed. The car was dusted unsuccessfully for fingerprints by the Florida Department of Law Enforcement, and then towed into the Volusia Country Sheriff's Office compound for safekeeping before it was removed to the Orlando Regional Crime Laboratory where it was analysed by Daniel Radcliffe.

The next find came on Wednesday, 13 December. Jimmy Bonchi and James Davis, who were out scavenging for scrap metal along a dirt road off Interstate 95, made a gruesome discovery. They had found Richard Mallory's corpse at a spot roughly five miles across the river from where his car had been discovered.

Volusia County deputies who responded to the 911 call saw a body that was skeletonised from the collarbone to the top of the head. Wild animals and insects had enjoyed a feast. The bulk of the putrefying corpse lay under a piece of cardboard with only the fingers showing. It was fully dressed in jeans and a pullover, the belt slightly askew. Detective James Malady, who arrived shortly after the body was called in, noted that the pockets of the jeans had been turned inside out. A set of dentures lay on the ground next to the corpse.

Charles James Lau, an investigator with the Volusia County Sheriff's Department, oversaw an immediate autopsy of the unidentified body and recovered four bullets from its torso. The hands of the victim were removed and transported to the crime laboratory for latent-print examination because, as Lau explained, 'When we have an unidentified body, you can't roll the fingerprints because of the decomposition.'

At Lee's trial, James Downing, the Daytona Beach medical examiner, described the removal of the body to a local funeral home on the night of 13 December. 'Ordinarily, bodies were sent to Halifax Hospital, but the decomposition of this body was too severe,' he said.

On the following day, the clothing was removed and sealed in a bag. 'I don't believe he had any underwear on,' Downing told the jury. 'I did not notice the zipper,' he added when questioned as to whether or not Richard Mallory's zip was closed or fastened. Dr Arthur Botting certified his death.

Several months of investigation into Mallory's sordid lifestyle and somewhat shady acquaintances produced no real leads. Police learned that he had last been seen at his shop on 30 November by Jeffrey Davis, the son of Jackie Davis, Mallory's last girlfriend. Officers were also able to locate a customer to whom Mallory confided his plan to visit Daytona Beach for a couple of days. Notes and phone numbers in the dead man's apartment led investigators to two dancers at local strip clubs, Chastity Marcus and Kimberly Guy, and Doug Lambert, Chastity's boyfriend.

Initial suspicion revolved around Chastity who was described as 'as hot as a firecracker' by the manager of the strip joint where she worked. She told the cops all about Mallory and his sick perversions. She introduced them to other girls who had been abused by this sexual pervert. Even Mallory's former girlfriend Jackie Davis told officers that he had been incarcerated for sex offences for ten years. But the cops slammed them all down and the case went cold.

By the middle of May 1990, the murder of Richard Mallory had been all but forgotten by the Volusia County Sheriff's Department. There was, seemingly, no reason to believe it was anything other than an isolated homicide.

Mallory's sister in Texas and his brother in New Jersey

wanted nothing to do with Richard's business. A Mr Townley took over the repair equipment that had been dumped, moved the shop several doors from the original site, and Mallory Electronics became Johnny's TV & VCR of Palm Harbor. Jackie Davis took charge of Mallory's cremation and scattered his ashes in nearby woodland.

But did anyone other than Lee know about the killing of Richard Mallory? In various quarters, it has always been accepted that Lee's lesbian lover had no knowledge at all of Mallory's murder. Indeed, after Lee's arrest for murder, Tyria initially told investigators that she had no inkling that Lee had been involved with any murder until they crashed murder victim Peter Siems's car on Wednesday, 4 July 1990 – almost a full seven months after Mallory was killed. She then watered down her story when pressed, saying that Lee had told her about the murder of Mallory but she didn't believe her.

Now, however, we can learn the shocking truth. Tyria knew about the murder of Richard Mallory because Lee had told her. In fact, she told her the very same day Lee had killed the man. Lee gave Tyria a scarf and jacket belonging to Mallory – it had 'Richard' printed inside the jacket collar – and she showed her a camera, a radar detector and toolbox which had mysteriously come into her possession. And, if all of this was not sufficient to raise Tyria's suspicions from non-belief to that of shock, she could have hardly failed to notice the blood-spattered car seat while she was driving round in Mallory's car for an hour.

Tyria would later say:

She [Lee] came home early one day in December with a two-door Cadillac with tinted windows and a gator plate [a Florida number plate] on the front. We used this car to move from Ocean Shores Motel to [an apartment on] Burleigh Avenue. Later that night after I came home from work, Lee told me she had shot and killed a guy that day. She later told me she had covered his body with a piece of carpet ... and left the car in some woods off John Anderson. And, when we moved in on Burleigh, she had gotten some things in which she showed me something with the name 'Richard' on it. She gave me a grey jacket and scarf, which I believe she had gotten from that car.

Richard Charles Mallory was shot to death very close to Ormond-by-the-Sea at around 5am on the morning of Friday, 1 December 1989, but now, for the first time, we can follow the sequence of events thereafter.

After blasting Mallory to death, Lee then drove his car to the Ocean Shores Motel in Holly Hill where she met up with Tyria. Using Mallory's Cadillac, together they moved their possessions to a low-budget or 'efficiency' apartment on Burleigh Avenue. They went back to their old apartment in the car, collected up their two pets – a dog and a cat – and returned to the new apartment. Tyria rode off on her moped, while Lee threw a 12-speed cycle into the back of the car and dumped the vehicle within a short distance of Burleigh Avenue where it was later found by police. She cycled back to the new apartment where she gave Mallory's grey jacket and scarf to Tyria, explaining in the same breath that she had 'shot and killed a guy that day'.

At 2.25pm on Wednesday, 6 December, Lee, using the alias of Cammie Marsh Green of 1 High Ridge Road, strolled into OK Pawn and Jewelry Inc, 305 Dr Mary McLeod Bethune Boulevard, Daytona Beach. She was about to pawn a Minolta Freedom camera and a Radio Shack Micronta Road Patrol Radar Detector, formerly the property of Richard Mallory. The ticket number 3325 recorded the transaction, and the manager, Linda Miller, handed over $35. Lee's obligatory thumbprint on the document would later prove part of her undoing.

The murder weapon was found after Lee's arrest. For four days police searched Rose Bay, and the rusty gun was located in the south-east corner between the sea wall and the first set of pilings supporting the bridge. Donald Champagne, ballistics expert and retired from the Florida Department of Law Enforcement, identified it as a .22-calibre, nine-shot pistol with six grooves and a right-hand twist. 'A popular weapon.'

There were no ballistic tests carried out on the weapon in an effort to match the casings and bullets with the revolver. The weapon was in such a bad state, the examiner would have risked serious injury had the gun been fired again.

Quite why police – in the full knowledge of Tyria's

conflicting statements and outright lies – chose not to prosecute her, at least as an accessory after the fact in the murder of Richard Mallory, we may only surmise. Had Tyria reported this murder to the police, at least seven other men would not have been shot to death. However, as later events will show, there was much more to this than meets the eye.

The jury did not know about Mallory and his predilections Of course, the last thing an attorney needs when prosecuting a woman accused of brutal murder, who is claiming self-defence, is for the court to learn the cold fact that the victim was a brutal, hard-drinking sexual deviant. Nevertheless, the truth is that many years back, in Anne Arundel County, Mallory had been confined in the Maryland penitentiary on the not insignificant charge of housebreaking with intent to rape.

Literally caught with his trousers down, and with mitigation in mind, Mallory entered a plea of insanity at his trial on Monday, 2 December 1957. The court ordered that a Dr Harold M. Boselaw examine him and the results make for grim reading: 'Mr Mallory possesses an extremely strong sexual urge along with a number of other neurotic manifestations with especially compulsive elements.'

Dr Boselaw's diagnostic opinion of Mallory was that he had a 'personality pattern disorder linked with a schizoid personality'. In layman's terms, he was an out-of-control compulsive sexual predator and pervert. But there is more.

Dr Boselaw summed up Mallory by adding, 'Because of his emotional disturbance and poor sexual impulses, he could present a danger to his environment in the future.'

In a nutshell, lady members of the jury, you would *not* want to hitch a ride with this guy, most certainly not without carrying a handgun – but the lady members of the jury knew nothing of this. However, this was not all the jury that held Lee's life in their hands did not know.

On Monday, 21 July 1958, Mallory had been committed to the maximum-security Patuxent Institute in Maryland for sex offenders as a defective delinquent for an intermediate period of time 'without maximum or minimum limit'. He would serve the best part of 11 years. Placing this punishment into a British perspective, a similar example would be one of confinement at Her Majesty's pleasure at either Rampton, Ashworth or Broadmoor Hospital for the Criminally Insane – home to the likes of Peter Sutcliffe and sundry other sexual psychopaths.

Mallory's file informs us that he 'exhibited argumentative behavior and engaged in a number of fights before adjusting to institutional life'. Nevertheless, after settling down and pushing a mop for a year, he wheedled his way into the somewhat cushy post of hospital clerk. This employment had the additional fringe benefit of bringing him into contact with female nurses. He was thrown out of this position on Monday, 22 August 1960, shortly after his arrival, because of his having made 'a molesting gesture towards the chart nurse with sexual intent'. He grabbed the young woman, fondled her breasts and pushed his hand up between her legs.

The trial jury was also unaware that a determined Mallory had further expressed his dissatisfaction at being detained by escaping from this maximum-security mental asylum on Tuesday, 14 March 1961. After trying to abduct a young girl, he was recaptured while driving a stolen car, and examined by a psychiatrist again. 'Mr Mallory is possessed with strong sociopathic trends, which are very close to his service, and his controls against them are weak and porous' was the painfully astute diagnosis. Mallory's custody file records that he remained quite successfully locked up until Tuesday, 16 April 1968, when he was released on licence. To his credit, he stayed well clear of the law thereafter.

Lee knew nothing of this when she accepted a ride in Mallory's car, and she knew nothing, and nor did the jury, of what is to follow.

In statements filed by Lee's attorneys at her appeal, it transpired that potential witnesses presented by her counsel were refused permission to testify as to Mallory's background. That he liked beating women, trading sex for his clients' electrical goods and generally being the best customer the sex bars had ever enjoyed cut no ice with the appellate judge at all. For example, Kimberly Guy had made a previous complaint to police that, in addition to having an affinity for prostitution and brutal sex, Mallory was equally interested in masochistic sex and that 'he frequently travelled with a pair of handcuffs in his briefcase'. In a nutshell, he had attacked her and all but strangled her to death. The officer who took her complaint knew that hookers were often on the receiving end of a john's bad temper. It came with the territory, so the cops left it that.

If Kimberly had been allowed to give her evidence at Lee's trial, the jury might have viewed him, and her claims of rape, in a different light. As Kimberly said, 'The cops, and I am not naming names here, knew all about Mallory and his filthy mind. If I had been Lee Wuornos under those circumstances, I would have shot him too.'

Chastity Marcus also made statements to the police about Mallory's crippling obsession with sex. She added, 'He would frequently exchange sexual favours for electronic equipment back at his shop.' Indeed, on one occasion both Chastity and Kimberly had three-way sex with Mallory. As payment for their services, Kim received a 19-inch colour television while Chastity took home a VCR – both items being the property of one of his trusting clients.

Of course, Lee knew none of this, and the jury, ignoring her desperate pleas that Mallory had raped her, lived in ignorance when they found her guilty of first-degree murder. But was Lee telling the truth? Did Mallory attempt to rape her that fateful night?

It was always claimed by the state's attorney that Lee murdered her victims for their money, and certainly all of her victims were carrying around $100 – sometimes substantially more, sometimes considerably less – when they were killed. To the often-penniless hooker, that was a lot of cash.

Lee has stated that she had been with more men than she could count – maybe more than 200 – although she once boasted to having laid 250,000 men (a preposterous exaggeration, for such a feat would require the bedding of 35 different males a day for about 20 years). More often than not, when down on her luck, she would charge less than the going rate to put a few dollars into her pocket. She has also made the point, not only to me but also to others, that when she was treated right, 'with respect', there was 'never a problem'.

Mallory had served a lengthy prison term of almost 11 years for breaking into a house and attempting to rape a woman. There were other charges left on the file that concerned violent sexual activity with females. However, what we don't know is how many other women, if any, failed to come forward and lay complaints against him. It has been claimed that, during the 21-year period since his release from Patuxent in 1968, Mallory had kept a clean sheet and had not come to the attention of the police for anything more than a few traffic violations. However, this good behaviour can be easily accounted for because he worked hard, and with cash in his wallet he satisfied his rabid sexual desires by using prostitutes, engaging in masochistic sex, using pornography, visiting strip clubs, drinking excessive amounts of alcohol and smoking drugs. In fact, the key to understanding Mallory's insatiable sex drive can be found in the simple fact that he had driven his business into bankruptcy through his headlong, uncontrollable pursuit of sex.

Mallory, a sexually aggressive loner, especially when fuelled by drink (and he drank to excess) was also excessively paranoid. He had a massive ego and considered himself a ladies' man. With huge debts piling up, verging on financial ruin, he did what so many men do in similar circumstances: he entered the world of sexual fantasy and escapism again and again. The rented false adoration of women kept his ego inflated, albeit at a high cost, while his world slowly collapsed.

With Mallory's temper still cooling from the long traffic delay, he saw Lee standing alone. The long, late-night drive, the booze, the intimacy of a warm car travelling the interstate, his financial worries forever creeping into his head, the conversation had to turn to sex once again. A deal was struck and then, with a flick of a switch, his alter ego came to the fore.

This time, however, he had chosen the wrong woman. This hooker was armed with a pistol, and she was prepared to use it. Sexually, mentally and physically abused from her formative years onwards, Lee was not the kind of woman to be hurt again, so she exploded into lethal violence.

'I've got respect for myself. Always did have. Weird, right?' she said to me.

It was a fatal mistake for Richard Mallory to treat her otherwise.

CHAPTER FIVE

DAVID SPEARS

MURDERED 19 MAY 1990

WE WERE GETTING NUDE AND EVERYTHING AND WE
WERE SCREWING AROUND AND ALL THAT STUFF,
GETTING DRUNK AND EVERYTHING AND, UH, THEN
HE... HE WANTED TO GO IN THE BACK OF THE TRUCK
AND ALL I REMEMBER IS THAT, I THINK THERE WAS
SOME KIND OF A LEAD PIPE OR SOMETHING LIKE THAT
AND WE WERE IN THE BACK OF THE TRUNK AND WHEN
I GOT BACK THERE, HE STARTED GETTING VICIOUS
WITH ME AND I JUMPED OUT OF THE TRUCK AND HE
JUMPED OUT OF THE TRUCK, RAN TO THE... TO THE
CAR, I MEAN, TO THE DOOR, OPENED THE DOOR,
GRABBED MY BAG, GRABBED THE GUN OUT, AND I
SHOT HIM... QUICK AS POSSIBLE. I SHOT HIM AT THE
TAILGATE OF THE TRUCK. AND THEN HE RAN AROUND
TO THE DRIVER'S SIDE TRYING TO GET IN THE TRUCK
TOWARDS ME, WHICH WAS WEIRD, TOWARDS ME, AND
I JUST RAN INTO THE TRUCK TOWARD HIM AND I

THOUGHT, WHAT THE HELL YOU THINK YOU'RE DOING, DUDE, YOU KNOW... YOU KNOW I... I AM GOING TO KILL YOU BECAUSE YOU WERE TRYING TO DO WHATEVER YOU COULD WITH ME. AND I SHOT HIM THROUGH THE... THROUGH THE DOOR AND THEN HE WAS KIND OF... WENT BACK AND I WENT RIGHT THROUGH TO THE DRIVER'S SIDE AND SHOT HIM AGAIN, AND HE FELL BACK. AND, THAT'S ALL I REMEMBER ON THAT ONE.

As ex-husbands go, 43-year-old David Spears was ideal. Practical, predictable, honest and hardworking, he was a man people counted on, the sort of guy you would want living next door to you. Earning his living as a construction worker, David lived in Winter Garden near Orlando, travelling south-west each day to Sarasota where he worked at Universal Concrete. A shy, softly spoken giant of a man, six foot four inches tall, bearded, greying and weather-lined from his outdoor lifestyle, he cared enough about his former wife, Dee, to give her a regular chunk of his monthly pay cheque. However, the thoughts going through David's mind on the day he picked up Aileen Wuornos were probably not so charitable.

The story of David's premature undoing begins just before lunchtime on Friday, 18 May 1990 when he called Dee and told her to expect him to call in some time between 2 and 2.30 the next day. On Saturday, he left work at about 2.10pm, a little later than planned, and started on his way in his old cream pickup north along I-75 to Tampa.

He headed north-east up I-4 and then hit US 27. He was not seen alive by anyone again – apart from his killer.

David spotted Lee somewhere near the point where US 27 intersects with I-4, about 26 miles south of Winter Garden, and offered her a ride. She explained that she needed to get to Homosassa Springs, which straddles US 19 on the state's west coast. Lee's destination was right out of David's way; in fact, it was at least 75 miles in the opposite direction to which he was heading. This was a 150-mile round trip and, as we recall, he had promised to meet with Dee around 2.30. More perplexingly, he would have had to pass within three miles of Winter Garden on the outward leg. Nevertheless, for some inexplicable reason, he agreed to take Lee.

Lee explained that they drove along US 27, then west on Highway 50, crossed I-75 on to Highway 90 and ended up pulling off the road on US 19 close to Homosassa Springs where David drove so deep into the woods 'he was worried that his truck would get stuck'. Whether we believe Lee's account of the murder or not, the facts are these: David Spears's truck was found abandoned ten miles west of Orange Springs near CR 318 and I-75 in Marion County on Sunday, 20 May; a blonde hair was found on the steering wheel and a ripped 'Trojan' condom packet was found on the floor of the vehicle; all his personal property, including tools, clothing and a one-of-a-kind ceramic statue of a panther which he had bought as a present for Dee, was missing. As in the previous killing of Richard Mallory, the driver's seat was pulled too close to the steering wheel for a man of his height, indicating to the police that someone else had driven the truck after the owner had been killed.

On Friday, 1 June, a man found the body of a male lying in a clearing amidst pine trees and palmettos. Mathew Cocking had just walked past an illegal dumping site on Fling Lane, a dirt road south of Chassahowitzka and running adjacent to US 19 in Citrus County, when he spotted the corpse. Mathew ran to the nearest payphone where he called 911.

When the police arrived, they found a badly decomposing body, nude except for a camouflage baseball cap which sat jauntily atop a ravaged head. On the ground near the body was a used Trojan condom, its torn black packet and several empty cans of Busch and Budweiser beer.

At first, because of the state of the body, the police were unable to determine the sex, age or likely cause of death. The corpse lay on its back, legs apart, arms outstretched, palms facing skywards. Lee had stolen her victim's wages, his daughter's graduation money and a quantity of cash he had hidden in his truck for emergencies amounting to about $600. She had hit pay dirt.

Dr Janet Pillow carried out the autopsy on Monday, 4 June. The man who weighed around 195 pounds in life had been reduced to 40 pounds by the time his body was discovered. Six .22-calibre bullets were recovered from the remains. Dental impressions identified the victim.

Everyone who knew Spears claimed that he could not and would not hurt a fly; he was incapable of the violent attack which his murderer would allege she had to defend herself against.

Five days later, another body was found.

CHAPTER SIX

CHARLES 'CHUCK' CARSKADDON

MURDERED 21/22 MAY 1990

THAT GUY, HUH, THE DRUG DEALER... HE HAD $20. HE WASN'T GOING TO GIVE ME ANY MORE MONEY. THE ONE WITH THE .45 ON TOP OF HIS HOOD. HE CRAWLED IN THE BACK SEAT AND I CRAWLED IN THE BACK SEAT AND HE SAID, 'YOU FUCKING BITCH' AND ALL THAT STUFF, AND I THOUGHT, YOU FUCKING BASTARD. I SHOT HIM IN THE BACK SEAT AND THEN I GOT OUT AND KEPT SHOOTING. I SHOT HIM MORE THAN... OVER NINE TIMES, BEAUSE I WAS PISSED WHEN I FOUND THE .45 ON TOP OF THE CAR.

In Great Britain, less than 20 per cent of serious crime and less than 10 per cent of murders are committed by women, in a society where they outnumber men. In the USA, only 12 per cent of murders are committed by women.

Ninety per cent of the victims of women who kill are

men, a statistic which speaks volumes. The vast majority of murders committed by women are, for want of a better phrase, crimes of passion. They are instigated by abuse or jealousy. Women generally are not as violent or physically aggressive as men, who may kill in brawls or during the course of crime. Without doubt there are different social controls on women which offer them less opportunity to be placed in a position to kill. It is a sign of the times, for instance, that they are not as free to roam the streets and bars at night. As we can see, Lee was an exception. Sometimes society and circumstance throw up a female killer who, because of the nature of her crimes and, indeed, because she is a woman, stuns and sickens us all. Lee Wuornos was that very rare specimen.

During the third week of May 1990, 41-year-old Charles 'Chuck' Carskaddon, a former road digger and rodeo rider, was en route from his mother's home in Boonville, Missouri, to Tampa to pick up Peggy, his fiancée. He had packed up the hard life and found less stressful employment as a press operator in his home state of Missouri. All he had to do was drive to Florida to collect Peggy, and his life would be complete. We may safely assume that he was driving south along the Dixie Highway when he spotted Lee thumbing a ride. In fact, chilling as it may seem, it is highly likely that, having dumped David Spears's truck close to I-75, one of the next rides Lee took was with Mr Carskaddon.

After they stopped – for sex, Lee claimed – she removed her gun from her bag and discharged no fewer than seven shots into the man's upper body from the back seat, claiming that it was an act of self-defence. After reloading her .22 she shot two more bullets into the corpse. The reason she gave for this cold-blooded and dreadful act was that she had found his .45-calibre handgun on the hood – or bonnet – of the car and was enraged to further violence by the thought that he may have planned to kill her.

Of the murder itself, we only have Lee's account above to inform us of the events that took place. At first she argued that the killing was in self-defence, then she changed her story, saying that she killed him just for the money. During the last few days of her life she told Nick Broomfield off-camera that she had, indeed, killed all of her victims in self-defence. Carskaddon's naked body was found 23 miles short of his destination on Wednesday, 6 June. The corpse was covered with foliage and a green electric blanket. The autopsy showed that he had been shot nine times in the chest with a .22-calibre handgun.

The dead man's brown 1975 Cadillac, a car he had lovingly restored, was discovered the next day around 45 miles north of where the body had been found, near I-75 and CR 484 in Marion County. Although the number plate had been ripped off, the vehicle identification number was still intact. A trace soon revealed the owner's name.

Carskaddon's mother, Florence, told police that when her only son left home he was carrying a blue-steel, .45-calibre pistol with a pearl handle, a Mexican blanket, a stun gun, a flip-top lighter, a watch and a tan suitcase. He was wearing a black T-shirt and grey snakeskin cowboy boots. 'He had removed the firing pin from the gun,' she said, 'because he was scared to use it.'

None of these items was found in his car, and Lee – minus a firing pin – was now packing more heat than ever before.

CHAPTER SEVEN

PETER SIEMS

MURDERED 7/8 JUNE 1990

OH, LET ME SEE... THIRD GUY... I HAD A PROBLEM WITH... UH... LET'S SEE... I THINK THE NEXT ONE'S THE ONE... HE WAS A CHRISTIAN GUY OR SOMETHING. I... I DIDN'T KNOW HE WAS A CHRISTIAN GUY. HE WAS NUDE... THIS IS THE ONE IN GEORGIA, I THINK, AND HE HAD HIS... HE HAD... HE TOOK A SLEEPING BAG... TOOK IT OUT IN THE WOODS AND WHEN WE GOT NUDE, I HAD TAKEN MY BAG WITH ME THAT TIME BECAUSE I SAID, 'WELL, IF WE'RE GOING TO GO OUT IN THE WOODS, I'M NOT GOING TO GIVE HIM AN OPPORTUNITY TO RAPE ME. AND THAT'S THE TIME THIS GUY GAVE ME A PROBLEM TOO. AND SO, I WHIPPED OUT MY GUN AND I SAID, 'YOU KNOW, I... I... I DON'T WANT TO SHOOT YOU.' HE SAID... HE DIDN'T SAY ANYTHING, HE JUST LOOKED AT ME AND SAID, 'YOU FUCKING BITCH.'

AND I SAID, 'NO, YOU WERE GOING TO RAPE ME.' BECAUSE HE WAS GETTING PHYSICAL WITH ME AGAIN AND I KNEW. AND HE... AND HE SAID, 'FUCK YOU, BITCH,' AND STARTED TO COME AT ME AND HE WAS, YOU KNOW, TRYING TO GET THE GUN FROM ME AND STUFF, WE'RE STRUGGLING ON THAT ONE. AND HE TRIED TO GET THE GUN FROM ME AND STUFF, WE'RE STRUGGLING WITH THE GUN AND EVERYTHING ELSE AND A COUPLE OF BULLETS SHOT UP IN THE AIR AND FINALLY I RIPPED IT AWAY AND I HAD THE GUN IN MY LEFT HAND AND I PUT IT BACK IN MY RIGHT HAND AND I SHOT HIM IMMEDIATELY... AND I'M POSITIVE THE ONLY ONE IN GEORGIA IS THE MISSIONARY GUY... I REMEMBER THE MISSIONARY GUY. I SHOT HIM ONCE.

Deeply religious, easy-going and considered a real gentleman in every respect, Peter Siems was a 65-year-old retired merchant seaman living on Florida's east coast near Jupiter, Martin County. He had found the Lord many years previously; soon he was to meet the Antichrist.

Early in the morning of Thursday, 7 June 1990 – the same day Carskaddon's car was found – neighbours saw the part-time missionary placing luggage and a stack of bibles into his 1988 silver-grey Pontiac Sunbird. They assumed, correctly, that the balding, bespectacled man was off on another of his trips to spread the word. On his travels, he intended to visit relatives in Arkansas and then drive up to New Jersey to see his sister. He promised his

MONSTER: MY TRUE STORY

wife that he would phone later in the day – she never heard from him again.

The most direct route for such a mammoth drive would be to join the Florida Turnpike near his home then cut up through the centre of the state until he joined I-75 near Wildwood, which was Wuornos country.

After her arrest, Lee admitted that she was very drunk when Siems stopped on I-95, though it was more likely to have been along I-75 where it crosses the Florida Turnpike in Marion County. She vaguely recalled crossing a state line in his car, but could not remember if it was Georgia or South Carolina. It was Georgia. She claimed that Siems 'became threatening during a sexual encounter in the woods, so I shot him'.

His body remains undiscovered. It lies rotting somewhere in the pinewoods of Georgia.

The mystery of the sudden disappearance of Mr Siems took a bizarre twist on Wednesday, 4 July when a silver-grey Pontiac Sunbird – not a red car as portrayed in the movie *Monster* – careered off CR 315 near Orange Springs, Florida, just ten miles east from where Lee dumped David Spears's truck. The car shot round a bend, skidded sideways and smashed through a steel gate and a barbed-wire fence, shattering the windscreen before coming to rest in the undergrowth. For a brief second it appeared that it might roll over, but it soon righted itself. With steam hissing from the radiator, and a slowly deflating tyre, the car, like its late owner, was doomed.

Rhonda and Jim Bailey, who were sitting on their porch drinking lemonade and enjoying the sun, witnessed the spectacular accident. Somewhat bemused, the elderly couple observed two women clamber out of the car. Lee, whose arms were bleeding from the cuts sustained in the crash, started throwing beer cans into the woods and swearing at her fellow passenger, who said very little.

The Baileys noted that the women grabbed a red-and-white beer cooler from the back seat and, still arguing, staggered off along the road. At the approach of other cars, they would dash into the woods and hide, only to reappear after the vehicles had passed. When the coast was clear, they returned to the car.

When neighbourly Rhonda ambled over to offer what little assistance she could, the blonde begged her not to call the police, saying that her father lived just up the road. The two women climbed back in the car and, with some difficulty, managed to reverse it on to the road and drive off. Within moments a front tyre went flat and, with the car now disabled, Lee and Tyria had no option other than to abandon it. They pulled off the rear number plate – Lee had done the same thing with Carskaddon's vehicle – and threw it, together with the car keys, into the woods before walking away.

A passing motorist, thinking that the women might need help, pulled over and offered assistance. He noticed that the blonde was not only bleeding but also very drunk. When she asked him for a lift, he thought better of it and refused, whereupon Lee became angry and abusive. The man drove away, but he phoned the Orange Springs Fire Department and told them about the injured woman.

Two emergency vehicles were dispatched to the scene and, when they arrived, Lee denied that they had been in the car. 'I don't know anything about any accident,' she snarled. 'I want people to stop telling lies and leave us alone.'

At 9.44pm, Trooper Rickey responded to the emergency call and found the car. (It was not until almost two months later that homicide detectives learned exactly where the Sunbird had first crashed, or heard the account given by Rhonda and Jim Bailey.) Marion County's Deputy Lawing was dispatched to investigate the abandoned, smashed-up vehicle. The vehicle identification number was checked, revealing that the missing Peter Siems was the owner. Bloody prints were found in the vehicle, and there were bloodstains on the fabric of the seats and on the door handles.

Items removed from the car by the police included Busch and Budweiser beer cans as well as Marlborough cigarettes and two beverage cosies. They were traceable to EMRO store number 8237, a Speedway truck stop and convenience store at SR 44 and I-75, close to the on-and-off ramps in Wildwood. The same EMRO store and truck stop would later feature in the murder of Charles Humphreys. Peter Siems and his wife were missionaries. They neither drank nor smoked, so the two beverage cosies did not belong to him. Underneath the front passenger seat lay a bottle of Windex window spray with an Eckerd drug store price label attached to it. This ticket was easily traceable to a store on Gordon Street in Atlanta, Georgia. Relatives also stated that the couple had never travelled to Atlanta but that Peter would probably pass close to the city en route to Arkansas.

Peter Siems had borrowed his son Stefan's suitcase for his trip. Stefan Siems later recognised it among the loot found in Lee's storage lock-up.

By now a police artist had drawn composites of the two women based on descriptions given by witnesses of the incident with the Sunbird. Armed with these sketches and the bottle of Windex, the investigators travelled to Atlanta to question the manager of the Eckerd drug store. Viewing the pictures, he recalled two women – identical to Lee and Tyria – entering his store on a Friday night. 'We are in a bad part of town in a predominantly black area, and white people do not venture into this area after dark,' he said. The police learned that the two women also purchased cosmetics and a black box of Trojan condoms – the same brand as those found near the body of David Spears and inside his car.

Fridays for June 1990 following Siems's murder fell on the 8th, 15th, 22nd and 29th respectively. On which of those days were the two women together in Siems's car when they purchased the Windex window spray, condoms and cosmetics in Atlanta? As Lee confirmed, she only drove to Atlanta once, and that was with Siems. She also confirmed that he was shot dead there. For her part, Tyria has denied ever travelling to Atlanta with Lee.

By the time 55-year-old Siems had reached the truck stop at Wildwood, he would have been tired and in need of a fuel top-up and refreshments. It is while here, I suggest, that he was approached by Lee and Tyria who had just purchased beer and the two cosies. From Wildwood, I suggest that the threesome – Siems, Lee and Tyria – headed north up I-75, crossed the state line into Georgia and continued on to Atlanta where they stopped at the Eckerd store. We know that the two women were at the Eckerd store on a Friday night because the manager identified them from composite drawings. Whether Siems was still alive at this point, or was murdered shortly afterwards, we may never know.

John Wisnieski of the Jupiter Police had been working on the case since Siems was reported missing. He sent out a nationwide Teletype containing descriptions of the two women, and he also sent a synopsis of the case, containing descriptions of the two females together with the sketches, to the *Florida Criminal Activity Bulletin*. Then he waited. He was not optimistic about finding Siems alive. The man's body had not been found, his credit cards had not been used and money had not been withdrawn from his bank account.

But what of the bloody fingerprints found in the wrecked Sunbird? The police knew that the owner of the car had vanished without trace – he had been reported as missing some three weeks *before* the crash on 4 July. A missing-person report had been circulated and a copy held on the Florida Department of Law Enforcement computer.

Now police had found the vehicle smashed up and two women had fled the scene in more-than-suspicious circumstances. But did the police run a fingerprint check through their own department at Orange Springs, or through the Florida Department of Law Enforcement? No, they did not.

CHAPTER EIGHT

EUGENE 'TROY' BURRESS
MURDERED 30 JULY 1990

HE PHYSICALLY ATTACKED ME... AND HE WAS... HE
LAUGHED. HE PULLED OUT A $10 BILL AND SAID,
'THIS ALL YOU FUCKING DESERVE, YOU FUCKING
WHORE'... LIKE THAT. AND I SAID, 'WAIT,' AND THEN
HE JUST... HE THREW THE FUCKING MONEY DOWN
AND I WAS STANDING IN FRONT OF THE TRUCK HERE,
AND HE HAD THE DOOR OPEN HERE, AND HE JUST
CAME... DIDN'T KNOW I HAD A GUN OR ANYTHING.
HE CAME AT ME. WE WERE FIGHTING. AND, UH, WHEN
I GOT AWAY FROM HIM, AND I RAN BACK TO THE
TRUCK, AND I HAD MY GUN IN THE BACK, AND I RAN
IN THE BACK REAL QUICK, AND HE... NOW, WE'RE
STILL FIGHTING, AND SOMEHOW HE... I KICKED HIM
OR SOMETHING. HE BACKED AWAY AND I PULLED MY
GUN OUT AND I SAID, 'YOU BASTARD,' AND I THINK I
SHOT HIM RIGHT IN THE STOMACH OR SOMETHING.

Ever-smiling Eugene 'Troy' Burress celebrated his fiftieth birthday in January 1990. A short, slightly built, blonde-haired man with a natural gift for the gab, he was employed as a part-time salesman for the Gilchrist Sausage Company in Ocala, a resort town in northern Florida where he lived with his wife Rose. Ocala is just 15 miles from Orange Springs, close to where the two women crashed Peter Siems's car.

Troy had formerly owned a pool-cleaning company, Troy's Pools, in Boca Raton on the south-east coast between West Palm Beach and Fort Lauderdale, but it went bust and the couple had moved to Ocala in 1989. Everyone liked Troy, who was now resigned to his new life. He had only one gripe: the lack of air-conditioning in his truck.

On Monday, 30 July 1990, Burress set out on Gilchrist company business. He would be travelling the Daytona route, which took him to several customers throughout central Florida. His last planned stop was to have been Salt Springs in Marion County, part of the extensive Indian reservation area and within a spit of Orange Springs where Lee and Tyria crashed Siems's Pontiac Sunbird, and close to where Lee dumped David Spears's truck.

When he failed to report at his office after work, Gilchrist manager Mrs Jonnie Mae Thompson was concerned. She started calling around the various customers and discovered that Burress had failed to show up for his last delivery. He had made the drop at Seville along SR 17; after that he vanished. Now Jonnie knew that something was very wrong. If he had broken down he would have phoned in, or used the American Automobile Association to help him out. He had done neither, so she immediately went out in search of him.

At 2am the following morning, Troy was reported missing by his wife. The police recorded her description of a slightly built man around five foot six inches in height and weighing about 155 pounds. He had blue eyes and blonde hair. This time there was a fast response with a quick, though tragic, outcome. At 4am Marion County deputies found the Gilchrist delivery van, distinctive with its black cab, white refrigerator back and company logo, on the shoulder of SR 19, 20 miles east of Ocala and within a few miles of Orange Springs. The vehicle was locked and the keys were missing, as was Troy Burress.

A family out for a picnic in the Ocala National Forest found Troy's body five days later, on Saturday, 4 August. They chanced upon his remains in a clearing just off SR 19, about eight miles from his abandoned delivery van. Florida's heat and humidity had hastened decomposition, precluding identification at the scene. However, he was confirmed as Troy Burress by his wife. She had given him the wedding ring he was still wearing.

Troy had been killed with two shots from a .22-calibre handgun, one to the chest and one to the back. A clipboard with delivery details and receipts, which had been removed from the van, was found near the body, but the company's takings were missing.

Lee later said, 'He took me to the woods and told me to

strip.' Then he offered her $10, sneering, 'That's all you're worth.' She claimed that he had sexually assaulted her, so she shot him in the chest. As he turned to escape, Lee shot him in the back. She made no secret that the second shot was deliberate: she seemed to be under the mistaken impression that a rape victim was legally justified in shooting a fleeing attacker.

CHAPTER NINE

CURTIS 'CORKY' REID
MURDERED 6 SEPTEMBER 1990

'CORKY REID. WHAT THE FUCK ARE YOU TALKING ABOUT?'

Curtis 'Corky' Reid's name is not generally mentioned alongside the life and crimes of Aileen Wuornos, mainly because the police investigating Lee's crimes were not in the least bit interested in his disappearance or subsequent death. Indeed, this is the one case where the police concerned with bringing Aileen Wuornos to justice should hang their heads in shame.

Corky had been a senior engineer at Cape Canaveral and had been through bad times. Twenty years before he vanished, he had plunged six storeys and survived, while others who had fallen from similar heights all died. Seriously injured, he had been cared for by his sister Deanie Stewart and her husband Jim who owned a car dealership. When he eventually returned to work, his wife had left him and now he was alone, living a sedentary lifestyle which revolved around the TV, Deanie and Jim. Every Sunday, without fail, he would call in to see his mother.

It was Thursday, 6 September 1990. Corky had just cashed his pay cheque and he called in to say that he was off for a long weekend to visit his friend Ray who lived at Cocoa Beach. He would then continue on to Orlando for an appointment with his doctor. He had experienced a slight stroke several months previously and needed a check-up, after which he would see his mum.

Corky kissed Deanie goodbye; she never saw him again.

On Sunday, 9 September, Deanie was surprised to receive a call from her mother. Corky had not arrived. At first there seemed to be no immediate reason for concern, but all that changed when, on Monday, Deanie got a call from her brother's secretary at the Cape. He had not turned up for work.

Deanie immediately visited Corky's home. His clothes and his badge were there, but there was no sign of her brother and his car.

Deanie and Jim's first port of call was the Titusville Police Department. The couple explained what was wrong and were advised to wait 72 hours before filing a missing-person report. This was the usual procedure in such circumstances, so the family took matters into their own hands. Within 48 hours, over 2,000 flyers were printed and sent out. Five hundred people went looking for the missing man in Brevard and Volusia Counties, but there were no responses.

Unlike all of Lee's other murder victims, whose trips had been lengthy, Corky's drive that Thursday should have been short and sweet. After leaving home, the drive to Cocoa Beach would have taken him just 15 minutes at best, then he would have headed out west on the Bee Line Expressway towards Orlando, a mere 25 miles away.

On Tuesday, 11 September, Corky's white two-door car was found, it is claimed, in a parking lot near the I-95. Deanie and her daughter Tina drove there immediately, expecting to find the Orlando Police at the scene. They were, in fact, met by the security guard for the parking lot. He explained that he was concerned because it had been there several days. He had called the police who, in turn, had called Tina.

So, there we have it. A man is reported missing, his car is found, and the police are informed yet they do nothing. With the great gift of hindsight, perhaps it would have been wiser to leave the car where it was until the police had given it the once-over. However, for reasons unknown, Deanie elected to drive the car back to their own parking lot, trying as hard as she could to preserve any fingerprint evidence en route.

When she arrived home, Deanie conducted a perfunctory search of the vehicle. Keys to the car and Cape Canaveral were on the floor, along with a torn Trojan condom pack and empty cartons of Marlborough and Camel cigarettes. The car, which Corky had regularly maintained in good working order, showed that there was no oil in the sump and little petrol in the tank. The brakes had been worn down. Someone had thrashed the car very hard indeed. Of even more significance was the fact that the glove compartment had been emptied out, although the registration papers remained. Corky's toolbox was missing and the driver's seat had been pulled forward, which indicated that someone shorter than the owner had driven the car. The NASA emblem had been scraped off the rear window – all the hallmarks of a Wuornos killing.

Corky's body has never been found.

Dan Carter of the Titusville Police Department took up the case but got nowhere despite it having all the signs of the serial-murder cases going on in the area. This lack of progress we cannot attribute to Dan Carter. He was told, in no uncertain terms, to back way off the case as soon as Lee and Tyria were located.

Totally frustrated, Deanie started calling the Marion County Sheriff's Department, demanding to know if any action was being taken on her brother's behalf. 'No one returned my calls,' she said. 'No one. They were always out in the field.'

Not one to be thwarted, Deanie called the attorney general and reported the non-action of the Marion County investigators. Soon afterwards, principal investigator Bruce Munster called her back.

'Does this call have anything to do with my call to the attorney general?' she asked.

'Yes, ma'am,' Munster admitted with some hesitation.

When she later learned that Lee had been arrested and Tyria had been brought back to Florida, Deanie asked Bruce Munster to show the women a photograph of her brother to see if they could identify him as a victim. Munster blatantly insisted that Curtis Reid was not one of Lee's victims.

'I didn't buy it then and I don't buy it now,' Deanie says.

Deanie's anger was further fuelled when she learned from one of Corky's friends at the Cape that the Marion County investigators had not been cooperating with other members of the task force. 'They told me that Dan Carter's name was not even on the task-force list,' she complained. She started to petition in an effort to force Munster to include Carter in the questioning of Aileen Wuornos:

We, the family of Curtis L. (Corky) Reid, ask for your help to sign this petition, so that Det. Dan Carter of the Titusville Police Department can question one Aileen Carol Wuornos now in custody, about the disappearance and possible death of Curtis L. (Corky) Reid. Mr. Reid disappeared Sept 6, 1990 from Titusville, Fl. where he has lived for the last 30 years.

'Within two days, I had received a phone call from Dan Carter asking me to pull the petitions in or Marion County would not cooperate,' she remembers.

To put a stop to all of this, Bruce Munster did have Corky's photograph to show both Lee and Tyria. He and his sidekick Larry Horzepa merely mentioned the missing man's name as an aside and only to Lee – who denied it all. After that, Corky's death was airbrushed into history. Or was it?

Shortly before Lee's trial for the murder of Richard Mallory, Deanie and Jim were invited to look at some property which was held at the Marion County Sheriff's Department. It had been confiscated from none other than Tyria Moore. 'My father's suitcase, which Corky had borrowed, was there. His Levi "Members Only" jacket was there. Sweatshirts like my brother wore – I recognised them all, but I couldn't prove they were his,' Deanie claimed. 'There were no identifying marks, but I knew they belonged to my brother.'

Bruce Munster explained in front of Dan Carter that, if Deanie could not 'positively identify the items', there was no more he could do.

At this stage in the investigation, it is worth mentioning that Munster and two of his colleagues were negotiating a movie deal to the tune of $100,000 each. Tyria was to receive considerably more. Individually, the items were of little significance. Collectively, along with the suitcase, they were damning evidence against Lee, and Tyria had already confided in Munster that Lee had given them to her.

Indeed, Tyria was to become quite a collector of dead men's property...

CHAPTER TEN

CHARLES 'DICK' HUMPHREYS
MURDERED 11 SEPTEMBER 1990

IF I MADE $130, I'D TAKE $30 AND GIVE HER [TYRIA MOORE] THE REST TO PAY THE BILLS. SHE ALWAYS TOLD ME, 'GET A MOTEL WITH A SWIMMING POOL, BECAUSE IT'S SO BORING HERE ALL DAY LONG.' SO I FOUND A PLACE WITH TWO SWIMMING POOLS, A SHUFFLEBOARD, A LOUNGE, AND A STORE WITH BEER... THE PROBLEM WAS I WASN'T SUPPORTING HER AS RICHLY AS SHE WANTED. SHE ALWAYS WANTED A BRAND-NEW CAR OR A RENTED ONE. SHE WANTED CLOTHES, SHE WANTED AN APARTMENT WITH PLUSH FURNITURE. 'I'VE GOT TO HAVE MY THINGS,' SHE SAID. SO MATERIALISTIC. I BROUGHT HOME ABOUT $300 EVERY TWO WEEKS, BUT IT WEARS YOU OUT, CONSTANTLY TALKING TO ALL THOSE MEN, STAYING UP.

A thoroughly decent chap, Charles Humphreys lived in the east-coast city of Crystal River, which is located about seven miles north of Homosassa along US 19, and he never made it home from his last day of work at the Sumterville office of the Florida Department of Health and Rehabilitation Services (HRS). Sumterville was right in the centre of Lee's territory.

Aged 56 years, he was a man of some experience who had formerly served as a police chief in Alabama. Now an investigator specialising in protecting abused and injured children, he was about transfer to the department's office at Ocala. He had three children, and his kindly nature made him an excellent choice to work with kids. He picked up his killer the day after his thirty-fifth wedding anniversary. His wife Shirley had been battling cancer for years.

'He was always in the driveway ten minutes after six,' Shirley recalled. 'At six-thirty, I thought it was car trouble. At seven, maybe he stopped for a beer. At eight, I panicked. I got the Highway Patrol ... The Wildwood Police Department started a search. The next day my son came. I sat and waited. I woke up at two-thirty the next night. I heard a knock on the door and knew right away what it was.'

It is claimed that on Tuesday, 11 September 1990 – the day Corky Reid's car was found abandoned near Orlando – Humphreys disappeared after picking up a hitchhiker, or hitchhikers, and the following evening his body was found off CR 484 within a stone's throw of where both Spears's and Carskaddon's vehicles had been found.

Charles had been shot seven times. Six .22-calibre bullets were recovered from his body, but the seventh copper-jacketed round had passed through his wrist and was never found. His money and wallet were missing. His trouser pockets had been turned inside out.

Humphreys's blue four-door Firenza car was found on Wednesday, 19 September some 70 miles to the north. It had been backed into a space behind an abandoned Banner service station at the intersection of I-10 and SR 90, near Live Oak in Suwannee County, and some 15 miles south of the state line with Georgia.

The number plate, keys and a bright yellow Highway Patrol Association bumper sticker had been removed from the car. During an initial examination of the vehicle, it was noted that everything which told the world it had belonged to Humphreys was gone or trashed – just like his life. Little things like his ice-scrapers, his maps, his personal papers, business papers and warranties. His favourite pipe in the newly carved wooden tray up on the dashboard was also gone.

By way of compensation, the killer left one can of Budweiser beer under the passenger seat. The police never dusted the can for prints.

Back at the police pound, a closer examination of the car's interior revealed a cash-register receipt for beer, or wine, from EMRO store number 8237, a Speedway truck stop and convenience store located at SR 44 and I-75 in Wildwood – the same store from which receipts were found in Peter Siems's car. The receipt was time-stamped

4.19pm, 11 September 1990, the day that Humphreys had disappeared. The clerk who had been on duty at the time could not identify the man but did recognise the composite police sketches of Lee and Tyria. When they left the store, the clerk believed they drove away and therefore did not call the police, as she was obliged to, because prostitutes are banned from truck stops throughout Florida.

Most of the victim's personal effects, including his pipe, pen and pencil, wedding ring and wristwatch – all covered with blood (Lee would claim that, after shooting him, she heard his gurgling moans and took pity on him by shooting him in the head to 'put him out of his misery') – were found a month later in a wooded field off Boggy Marsh Road, around 18 miles from where his body was found in southern Lake County near US 27. They were returned to his wife.

On the face of it, this murder seems much like the previous killings: a lone woman is picked up while hitchhiking; she kills the driver and robs him. However, on this occasion, all is not as it seems.

As an investigative criminologist, my work often demands that I look laterally at criminal investigations. Tyria Moore has always denied knowing anything about Lee's crimes and the public have always believed this to be the case. But Tyria had been riding around with Lee in Peter Siems's car, and we know this because she was driving the vehicle when it crashed near Orange Springs.

The girls had been drinking prior to the accident on the nearby Indian reservation. We also know all about Tyria riding around in Richard Mallory's car and accepting his property; and the property of Corky Reid was found in her possession.

This brings us back to Charles Humphreys. It is known that he left his office in Sumterville on 11 September and was driving west towards his home in Crystal River, when he stopped to give a blonde woman a ride – Lee and Tyria were certainly at the EMRO store around the same time as Humphreys drove past. His obvious route was to leave his office, drive north to Wildwood, cross I-75 and head home along SR 44. What we now know is that at around 4pm he pulled into the EMRO store number 8237 in Wildwood.

On this occasion, the EMRO clerk recalled two women purchasing beer or wine – evidence found later showed it was cans of Budweiser and bottles of Miller Lite. The women bore striking similarities to Lee and Tyria. The clerk was unable to identify the male who had been driving the car, but he could only have been the soon-to-be deceased because the two women climbed into the car.

Police evidence reveals that this man's body was found in one of Lee's favourite dumping grounds, along CR 484, the day following his murder. The distance from the truck stop to where he was shot to death was about 20 miles – maybe 15 minutes' driving time at best.

The scenario can only be that Lee and another woman,

who has never been positively identified, were hitching a ride and Humphreys stopped his car. Within a short distance after leaving work he picked up the two women then met his death.

Tyria denied any knowledge of being in the dead man's car that day; she said she knew nothing of the murder until police later questioned her about Lee's movements. She claimed never to have met anyone called Charles Humphreys, but she was unable to account for her movements during the time in question.

In an affidavit following Lee's arrest, Tyria described what had happened during the last few months she was with Lee:

She came home with an older pickup truck – David Spears's vehicle – approximately late May or early June 1990, and a day or two later came home with an older brown car – Charles Carskaddon's 75 Cadillac.

The next car she came home with was a Pontiac Sunbird – Peter Siems's car – which she told me a couple of stories of where she had gotten it approximately in June of 1990. At that time, she showed me approximately $600 in cash in $100 bills. She later took myself and my sister to Sea World.

She kept the car until July 4, when I was driving it back through a dirt road to see an Indian reservation. On the way back out, I lost control and rolled the car through a gate and a fence. We got out and Lee told me to run. At that time, I thought the car might blow up.

A couple of people came out and Lee told them not to call the cops because her father lived just down the road. We then returned to the car and Lee tore off the license plate from the back and threw it in the field. She then got in the driver's seat and I got in the back seat and she drove until the tire went flat. When we got out, she tore the plate off the front of the car and threw it into a field. We then ran to a wooded area and at that time I knew the car must have been stolen.

In the wooded area, Lee washed some blood off herself which she had gotten when the car rolled over and had got cut on some glass on her right arm. We then went on down the road and at some time she threw the keys and the registration into a field or woods.

We were approached by a couple of people whom I believe were with a fire department or something like that. They asked if we were the ones in the wreck and Lee said no and I agreed.

We went down the road to a house where a gentleman gave us a ride to State Road 40. We were then picked up by a lady with kids and she gave us a ride to what I believe was a store. That was as far as she was going. There was a road that went back off of 40.

We were then picked up by a gentleman who took us to some kind of military base where we all went in. We had to give our names. Lee said a name for me and I gave my last name. After leaving there, the gentleman gave us a ride all the way to Daytona Avenue behind our house in Holly Hill.

The next car I saw Lee with was a 4-door small blue car – Charles Humphreys's property – in approximately late August to early September 1990. I came in from Casa del Mar and Lee was on the bed with a couple of briefcases and some boxes going through it. We later drove to Bellair Plaza where we threw something away in a dumpster.

A day or two later, I heard the news of the murder and they [the police] showed me a picture of the dead man's car, which was the same one Lee had.

Tyria left her job at the Casa del Mar Motel, and in the fall of 1990 they moved into room number 8 at the Fairview Motel at Harbor Oaks on US 1 along Daytona Beach. Tyria was unemployed and the two women were living off Lee's earnings.

The staff at the local convenience store got to know Lee and Tyria as regular, sometimes troublesome, customers. Brenda McGarry recalled that Lee would often approach men in the 50-to-60 age range while they topped up their cars with petrol. 'She was very masculine and aggressive,' she said. 'Always flexing her muscles and talking about needing to get over to 92, which I thought was a bar or something. It never registered that it was a highway.'

The owners of the Fairview soon tired of them and once again they moved, this time to the nearby Belgrade, a

Yugoslavian restaurant owned by Velimir Isailovic and Vera Ivkovich. Vera allowed the women to rent a room at the rear of the premises for $50 a week. Then the problems started.

Contradicting Lee's later statements to police that Tyria rarely drank and was as pure as the driven snow, Vera confirmed that, 'Lee and Tyria were drunk most nights ... they invaded the quiet dignity of the Belgrade restaurant, night after night singing and making a racket in their room, their loud music upsetting the customers.'

In his deposition, Velimir Isailovic recounted bad times:

Two, three days after she [Lee] check in she said, 'Can you give me a ride to my job?'

I said, 'OK.' Because she don't have car. She don't have nothing. She stay in the room. She gave money if she go to work. Put her in my pickup truck. Say, 'Which way are you going to go?'

She says, 'Going south to the New Smyrna Beach.'

And I ask her, 'Do you know where you are going to go, do you know the street address?' Because she tell me she got cleaning business. I think she is going to go somewhere to clean house or something like that.

She say, 'Keep going.'

I start to laughing, I say, 'I think, you don't know where you are going to go.'

She say, 'I know, turn right to the 95.'

I say, 'Why don't you tell me, I don't have gasoline to go too far.'

She say, 'OK, if you catch 95, exit south and stop.'

Again, I don't have in my mind nothing wrong. I ask, 'How are you going to go from here?'

'Don't worry, I'm walking.'

I drop her on 95 exit south. I come back home and I tell my wife, 'Look she don't have any business. She does not work anywhere. You know where I put her? Right on 95. Some kind of monkey business, yet.' But what kind we don't know, I don't know. I don't know how long she going to stay out that day, that time. Probably several hours. Not too long.

Three, four, five hours she come back. She bring – give my wife very small money, $30, $40. I don't know. Not too much. She go in the room, buy beer, drink beer all night long. I say, 'I don't know how come she has got money to buy beer, but she don't have money to pay the rent and food.' Start to make me really mad and confused.

But, anyhow, I quit to give her any favour. She say, 'What's wrong with you?'

I say, 'Nothing at all, you start to lie, you don't have any job, you don't have any business.'

'Oh yes, I got good business, good for this and that, can you give me a ride?'

I say, 'No. I told you no any favour for you any more.'

She say, 'Can you give me ride to Winn-Dixie store?'

Said, 'No.'

She start to bring $10, $20 to my wife. I say, 'That's enough. Better tell her to go out.' That's three weeks.

Two or three days before Thanksgiving, I think. The other girl left first.

Now, with both women's composites plastered across newspapers and screened on TV, Tyria bailed out. She went home for Thanksgiving and Lee left their lodgings on 10 December, begging and borrowing her way back into the Fairview Motel.

'Several times she [Lee] tried to give me things,' Vera recalled. Once it was an electric razor, and again a gold chain. Several days after they went, Velimir saw Lee in the gas station.

'Just make joke, I say, "Hey, when you bring me my money?" because she now owed $30 or $40.

'And, that time she say, "I'm sorry, you are son of a bitch, you are lucky you are still have life."'

Shortly after this incident, Vera and her husband saw two photofits in the local paper and immediately recognised the faces as Tyria Moore and Aileen Wuornos. They called the cops.

By now, investigators should have been taking careful note of the cluster of incidents that were taking place around the small area of the Seminole Indian Reservation area in the Ocala National Forest, but they did not. David Spears's abandoned truck had been found close by. Peter Siems's Pontiac Sunbird had crashed at Orange Springs. Troy Burress had failed to make his last delivery in the area; his van had been found abandoned along SR 17 and his body had been dumped in the forest.

However, if all these coincidences were not enough to galvanise the authorities into action, the discovery of yet another abandoned car at almost the very same spot along CR 484 where Lee had left Carskaddon's vehicle should have been a loud wake-up call.

CHAPTER ELEVEN

WALTER GINO ANTONIO

MURDERED 17 NOVEMBER 1990

WHEN WE WERE STRUGGLING WITH THE GUN AND
EVERYTHING ELSE, AGAIN, HE FELL TO THE GROUND
AND HE STARTED TO RUN BACK... RUN AWAY. AND I
SHOT HIM IN THE BACK... RIGHT IN THE BACK. HE
JUST KIND OF LOOKED AT ME FOR A SECOND AND HE
SAID... HE SAID SOMETHING LIKE, UH... SHIT. WHAT
DID HE SAY? I THINK HE SAID, 'YOU CUNT,' OR
SOMETHING LIKE THAT. AND I SAID, 'YOU BASTARD,'
AND I SHOT HIM AGAIN.

By now, a number of law-enforcement officers investigating
the various murders were starting to collate their
evidence. Marion and Citrus County detectives had
compared notes on the Burress and Spears killings. Then
they spoke to Detective Tom Muck in Pasco County after
they read in the Florida Department of Law Enforcement

bulletin that Muck's victim might be linked to Spears. That made three bodies, indicating that a serial killer was at large.

The crimes had a number of features in common, including the fact that the victims were all older men who had been robbed, and two of them had had their pockets turned inside out. All three killings had been carried out using a small-calibre weapon. Bullets recovered from the bodies were .22-calibre, copper-coated and hollow-nosed, with rifling marks made by a right-twist firearm.

Another link emerged when the police exchanged the composite sketches made by their individual witnesses. They bore significant similarities, suggesting they were looking for the same short, blonde woman. If she was a sole killer, and not working with a man, the officers reasoned, then she might well use a small handgun.

Captain Steve Binegar, commander of the Marion County Sheriff's Criminal Investigation Division, knew about the Citrus and Pascoe Counties murders. He could not ignore the similarities between the murders, and had begun to formulate a theory.

Steve's first job was to form a multi-agency task force with representatives from the counties where the bodies were found. 'No one stopped to pick up hitchhikers in those days,' he said, 'so the perpetrator of those crimes had to be initially non-threatening to the victims. Specifically, when I learned that two women had walked away from Peter Siems's car, I looked at the Trojan brand of prophylactics. Then came the composites and the truck-stop clerk. Then I said to the other guys, "We've got to be looking for a highway hooker, period."'

Steve Binegar decided to turn to the press for help. In late November, Reuters ran a story about the killings, reporting that the police were looking for two women. Newspapers throughout Florida picked up the story and ran it, along with the sketches of the women in question. In every respect they matched Aileen Wuornos and Tyria Moore – *both* women were now suspects in a serial-homicide case.

We can gain a tremendous amount of information from the men who met Lee and were lucky to escape with their lives.

In November 1990, and the date is uncertain, trucker Bobby Lee Copus was driving his car from his home at Lakeland along I-4 to Orlando to pay an insurance bill, a trip of about 45 miles. En route, the heavy-set man in blue jeans pulled into a truck stop near Haines City, some 24 miles south-west of Orlando. Here he met Lee who said that she needed a ride to Orlando. She told the trucker she needed to get to Daytona Beach by a certain time to pick up her two children at a day-care centre. Once in Orlando, she said, she would call her sister for a ride the rest of the way home.

Copus drove to his bank, withdrew approximately $4,000 for his insurance bill and tucked the money into his sun visor. He continued to Orlando along a country road. Lee was soon to proposition the man, asking for $100 with the promise of giving him the best blowjob he had ever had in his life. Copus, who was happily married, had no intentions of cheating on his wife so he declined. Twice more Lee propositioned him, insisting that he stop in an orange grove. Again he refused, and Lee became angry.

Speaking in a thick cowboy drawl as he gave evidence at Lee's trial, Copus said, 'When she propositioned me for the third time, she wasn't the same person. She opened her purse for a comb. I'd seen what I thought was a small-calibre pistol in her purse. At this point I was really scared. I just wanted her out of my car in the presence of a lot of people.'

Copus was not as dumb as he may have appeared and he gambled on a trick which saved his life. He stopped at a truck-stop payphone and, after telling Lee he would drive her all the way to Daytona Beach, gave her $5 to call her 'sister'. As soon as she climbed out of the car, he slammed the door closed and locked it. Lee flew into a rage. 'What I saw was a woman in total frustration, mad as hell,' Copus recalled.

As he sped off in a cloud of dust, she screamed after him, 'Copus, I'll get you, you son of a bitch! I'll kill you like I did the other old fat sons of bitches!'

It is highly probable that the next man who stopped to give Lee a ride, more than likely the very same day, was Walter Gino Antonio.

Hailing from Merritt Island, Cocoa Beach – near Cape Canaveral, along the east coast of Florida – 60-year-old

Walter Gino Antonio was a trucker who doubled as a reserve police officer in Brevard County. On Saturday, 17 November, he was driving to Alabama in search of a job. Recently engaged, he wore a gold and silver diamond ring, a gift from his fiancée. It was a size 10 ¾, yellow gold with a diamond set in a field of white gold. When Tyria arrived back in Florida after Thanksgiving, Lee gave her this ring as a gift to prove how deeply she loved her.

Walter's obvious route was more or less identical to that of the late Peter Siems. He would use the Florida Turnpike as far as Wildwood then head upstate along I-75, probably pulling into the Speedway truck stop before the long haul north.

On Sunday, 18 November, a police officer out hunting game found a man's body, naked except for a pair of socks, near the intersection of US 19 and US 27 – 15 miles south of Wildwood. Walter Antonio had been shot four times, three times in the torso and once in the head, with a .22-calibre handgun.

After the murder, Lee drove the car back to the Fairview Motel where she asked the manager, Rose McNeill, if she could park her 'boyfriend's car' behind the building. She was told that the boyfriend was married and he did not want to have his wife drive by and find his car parked at the motel. Mrs McNeill recalled that Lee left the car there for just a few days. The maroon Pontiac Grand Prix was found on Saturday, 24 November in a wooded area near I-95 and US 1 in northern Brevard County, 20 miles south from where he started his journey. The number plate and keys were missing and a bumper sticker had been removed. A piece of paper had been crudely pasted over the vehicle identification number, and the doors were locked.

A number of empty Budweiser cans were found on the ground near the vehicle, which had been wiped clean of fingerprints.

Detectives learned that Antonio meticulously recorded every purchase he made of car fuel, retaining the filling-station receipts on which he noted his mileage. From this methodical behaviour, they were able to deduce that, in the week since his disappearance, his car had been driven over a thousand miles.

Walter's fiancée gave the police a list of possessions that had been in his car, including handcuffs, a reserve-deputy badge, a police billy club, a flashlight, a Timex wristwatch, a suitcase, a toolbox and a baseball cap. All of these items were missing. Walter Antonio's personal identification and clothing were discovered in a wooded area in Taylor County. The rest of his property has not been found.

Lee would later claim that she was out looking for custom as a hooker when Antonio pulled up. She asked if he wanted to help her make some money, but he pulled out his police badge and threatened to arrest her unless he got a 'free piece of ass'.

Under interrogation by officers, she was asked how many times did she shoot Antonio.

'Twice, I think.'

'OK. Now how did you feel when you thought he was a cop?'

'At first, I... because that one guy, that HRS guy telling me he was a cop, I said to myself, this... he's a... that guy was an HRS guy. So this is another faker. He's just trying to get a piece of free ass. And that's all I thought. Yeah, it pissed me off.'

'Well, when you shot him the first time, what did he do?'

'Mmm, well, when we were struggling with the gun and everything else, again, he fell to the ground and he started to run back... run away. And I shot him in the back... right in the back.'

'What did he do then after you shot him in the back?'

'He just kind of looked at me for a second and he said... he said something like, uh... shit. What did he say? I think he said, "You cunt," or something like that. And I said, "You bastard," and I shot him again.'

In just over a year, Lee Wuornos had scattered a trail of middle-aged male corpses across the highways of central Florida.

PART THREE

'AND MAY GOD HAVE MERCY
ON YOUR CORPSE.'

CHAPTER TWELVE

PARTING COMPANY

'When she went looking for someone to kill out there on those roads, it was her daddy she was really seeking to hurt.'

CAPTAIN STEVE BINEGAR,
ARRESTING OFFICER

Following Captain Steve Binegar's appeal for information through the newspapers, calls began to pour in and, by mid-December 1990, detectives had a number of firm leads involving the two women suspects.

A man in Homosassa Springs, where Lee asked David Spears to drop her off, said that two women who fitted the composites had rented a recreational vehicle (RV) mobile home from him about a year earlier. After searching through his records, he came up with the names of 'Tyria Moore' and 'Lee'.

A witness in Tampa said two women had worked at her

motel south of Ocala, close to where Troy Burress was murdered. Their names, she said, were Tyria Moore and Susan Blahovec, and they let it be known they had bought an RV in Homosassa Springs. The informant remembered that the blonde Blahovec was the dominant of the duo, and she believed she was a truck-stop prostitute. She also told the police that both were lesbians.

The information from these two callers rang immediate alarm bells with the task force. David Spears, Homosassa Springs, RV trailer, two women. Troy Burress, Ocala, RV trailer, the same two women. The investigation was starting to pay off as previously tenuous links started coming together.

Meanwhile, the composite sketches published by the media of the red-lipped blonde with the stringy hair and her dark-haired, moon-faced companion in the baseball cap had been haunting Tyria for weeks. On Friday, 23 November, the day after Thanksgiving, Tyria returned to Florida where the two women met at the airport. Lee was accompanied by a friend called Donald Willingham who had given her a lift. Don had met Lee in a bar the previous year. They had played pool, shared a few drinks and gone their separate ways.

The plane arrived just after noon. Lee presented Tyria with Walter Gino Antonio's engagement ring as a token of her love, and Don gave the women a ride back to the Fairview Motel where Lee asked him if he could come back a few days later to help them move their belongings. They were being evicted again. Lee pleaded with Tyria not to leave and, as another display of her love, the serial killer threw her nine-shot .22 into the brackish water of Rose Bay.

Upon his return on 3 December, Don asked the two women where they were going with their boxes and suitcase. 'I guess we'll have to put it in storage,' said Lee, before explaining that her girlfriend was going back up north and they were splitting up.

Don took the women to the Greyhound bus station in Daytona where Tyria handed back the ring and they tearfully parted company. From there, he drove Lee to Jack's Mini-Warehouse on Nova Road, where she deposited several cardboard boxes. The owners, Jack and Alice Colbert, rented the bin to Lee who was using the alias Cammie Greene. The cupboard, in building 43, hall number 1, bin G, was paid up until February.

From Jack's Mini-Warehouse, they drove to Don's house and had sex in bed.

'In going to bed with her, did she charge you money?' Willingham was asked during his deposition.

'No. She didn't charge me any money. I had been hauling her around. As a friend, really,' he said.

Lee wheedled her way back into Rose McNeill's affections and back into the Fairview Motel, asking to be moved into another room because number 8 held too many painful memories. Her possessions had now dwindled to a tan suitcase and the single key which opened the storage locker at Jack's Mini-Warehouse.

At 12.05pm on Friday, 7 December, Lee, still using the

alias Cammie Marsh Greene, once again visited the OK pawn shop in Daytona Beach. Her ticket, number 7529, shows that she received a paltry $20 for Walter's engagement ring.

Now aged 34, but looking considerably older, Lee was mentally and physically almost washed up. Pining for her lost lover, she spent days on end brooding in her room. Out of money and not tricking, she had to leave. She took to the streets, sleeping where she could. If she found a john, and business was good, she would have the money to get a motel room for the night. However, business was not always good and life for Lee Wuornos had reached rock bottom.

The breakthrough for the investigators came from Port Orange near Daytona. Local police had picked up the trail of the two women and were able to provide a detailed account of the couple's movements from late September to mid-December.

They had stayed, primarily, at the Fairview Motel in Harbor Oaks near Ormond-by-the-Sea where Lee registered as Cammie Marsh Greene. They spent a short time in a small apartment behind the Belgrade restaurant near the Fairview, but returned later to the motel. Then Wuornos, aka Blahovec, aka Greene, returned alone and stayed until 10 December. A national police computer check gave driver's-licence and criminal-record information on Tyria Moore, Susan Blahovec and Cammie Marsh Greene. Tyria Moore had no record worth considering, breaking-and-entering charges against her in 1983 having been dropped.

Blahovec had one trespassing arrest, while Greene had no record at all. Additionally, the photograph on Blahovec's licence did not match the one for Greene.

The Greene ID was the one that finally paid off. Volusia officers checked pawn shops in the area and found that Cammie Marsh Greene had pawned the 35mm Minolta Freedom camera and a Micronta Road Patrol Radar Detector (both items owned by Richard Mallory). Few people even own a Radio Shack Radar Detector, so this combination sparked the detectives' interest. In Ormond Beach, Lee had pawned a set of tools that matched the description of those taken from David Spears's truck, although the police failed to recover these.

The thumbprint on pawn ticket number 3325 proved to be the key. Jenny Ahearn of the Florida Department of Law Enforcement's Automated Fingerprint Identification System found nothing on her initial computer search, but not one to be put off, she visited Volusia County with colleagues where they began a hand search of fingerprint records.

Within an hour, the team struck gold. The print showed up on a weapons charge and outstanding warrant against a Lori K. Grody. Her fingerprints matched a bloody palm print found in Peter Siems's Sunbird. All of this information was sent to the National Crime Information Center, and responses came from Michigan, Colorado and Florida confirming that Lori K. Grody, Susan Blahovec and Cammie Marsh Greene were all aliases for one person: Aileen Carol Wuornos.

By now, Tyria was keeping her head down and was back living with her parents in Ohio. Lee was living rough when, on Wednesday, 19 December, she met a paunchy ex-marine named Dixie Mills at Wet Willie's Bar on US 1. Both were drunk, and they shared a common reason to get plastered: Lee was grieving over her loss of Tyria, while Dixie was shattered because his wife had left him after just a few months of marriage.

Mills would later recall that Lee was a very intelligent woman. 'We talked about a lot of things – from art to parapsychology to ancient history. I couldn't believe I'd met another human being that had such awesome comprehension and knowledge.' He found Lee to be a 'wild, savage party animal' with an insatiable desire for sex and alcohol. 'There's only two people I've ever met who have met the devil and shaken his hand,' boasted Mills. 'The one is me and the other is her.'

The two hellraisers stayed together until Christmas Eve, when Mills left Lee to return to his wife. On parting, he gave her $50.

Almost a year later, Mills recounted an entirely different story to the *Globe* newspaper.

'It all started so innocently. But it turned into a nightmare. If I'd known what I was getting myself into, I would have run for my life. But I didn't have a clue. On that first day, I was trying to drown my sorrows in beer at Wet Willie's in Daytona Beach, and I saw this woman doing exactly the same thing down at the other end of the bar ... that night, her troubles made her all the more appealing. We were both pretty down and out, and we desperately needed each other. Suddenly, she turned, looked deep into my eyes and said, "Dick, you and I are one – aren't we."'

Several days later, he said that Lee made him an offer. 'Dick, I'll be your wife if you pay me $500 a month.'

Mills went on to claim that he was 'stunned', and no way would he ever do such a thing. And, according to him, she revealed many of her secret fantasies, one of which entailed her being hooded while she was tied to a tree in a forest. Then 'a guy would come up to her and rape her, and then shoot her in the head'. She told him that the killing would make her climax.

Apparently, and this is Mills's side of the story, he took her to two family parties – one at Christmas and the other at his daughter's house in Ohio. 'On both occasions, she got blind drunk and insulted everybody. After that I offered her $500 if she stayed out of my life.'

Lee dismissed all of this to me, saying, 'Yeah, I remember the guy. I stayed with him and he paid me for sex. He gave me $50 plus a few beers. I never went to no parties with him because he left me to get with his wife over Christmas. He was crying like a kid over his wife. Never met his daughter either. What man is going to introduce a hooker like me to his daughter when he is trying to get back with his wife? It is all bull.'

CHAPTER THIRTEEN

THE ARREST

Posing as leather-clad bikers, two under-cover detectives, Mike Joyner and Dick Martin, finally spotted Lee Wuornos at 9.19pm on Tuesday, 8 January 1991 and kept her under surveillance. A police report describes the events that led to her arrest.

A surveillance team was dispatched to the Daytona Beach area in search of Aileen Wuornos and Tyria Moore. On 01/08/91 a team of Officers inside the 'Port Orange Pub' on Ridgewood Avenue, Daytona, spotted Wuornos at that location. Undercover Officer Mick Joyner observed her with a tan suitcase which she carried from one location to another. Conversations with her and the observations of the undercover team were that she has mood swings from friendly and congenial to aggressive and abusive and is known to consume both Busch and Budweiser can beer and smoke Marlborough cigarettes. She told Mike Joyner that everything she had was in the suitcase and showed a key to him which she said was her life. (This was the key to her lock-up at the storage warehouse.) She then walked to the Last Resort Bar (where she had been sleeping rough on a yellow vinyl car seat outside of the premises). She spent the night in the bar with this suitcase. She hadn't any place to stay and told Joyner that she had broken up with her girlfriend, Ty, and missed her. The surveillance continued until the evening hours of 01/09/91 at the Last Resort Bar. Intelligence revealed a large party was to occur at the bar that evening. Because of this, a decision was made that surveillance would be almost impossible.

So, the serial killer was drinking at the Port Orange Pub on Ridgewood Avenue in Harbor Oaks, about half a mile north of her favourite bar, The Last Resort, one of the many biker bars that line US 1. But the official police report does not indicate that their carefully planned operation to catch Aileen Wuornos almost went disastrously wrong.

While she was in the Port Orange Pub, two uniformed Port Orange police officers – to the dismay of the undercover cops – walked into the bar and took Lee outside. Joyner and Martin frantically telephoned their command post at the Pirate's Cove Motel where authorities from six jurisdictions had gathered to bring the investigation to a head. They concluded that this development was not a leak but simply a case of alert police officers doing their jobs. Bob Kelly of the Volusia County Sheriff's Office called the Port Orange police station and told them not to arrest Lee under any circumstances. The word was relayed to the officers, who suddenly had a more pressing engagement to attend to, and Lee was allowed to return to the bar.

The action now shifted back to the two undercover detectives who struck up a conversation with Lee and bought her a few beers. She left the bar at around 10pm carrying a leather suitcase and declining the offer of a lift. Once again, the cautious arrest was almost ruined when two Florida Department of Law Enforcement (FDLE) officers pulled up behind Lee, following her with their lights off as she walked down Ridgewood Avenue. Police at the command post radioed the FDLE officers to back off, allowing Lee to proceed to The Last Resort.

Joyner and Martin met her at The Last Resort, drinking and chatting until midnight when she left. But she did not go far: Lee Wuornos spent her last night of freedom sleeping on an old yellow vinyl car seat under the tin-roof overhang of the bar.

Surveillance was planned to continue throughout the following day, but, when the police learned that a large number of bikers were expected for a party at the bar that evening, they decided further surveillance would be impossible. By simply donning a crash helmet, Lee could quite easily disappear among the hundreds of motorcyclists milling around at the party, and vanish for good. The decision was made to go ahead with the arrest.

Joyner and Martin asked her if she would like to use their motel room to clean up before the party. At first she was reluctant, but then she changed her mind and left the bar with them.

Outside, on the steps leading to the bar, Larry Horzepa of the Marion County Sheriff's Office approached Lee and told her that she was being arrested on an outstanding warrant for Lori Grody, one of her many aliases. This related to the illegal possession of a firearm and no mention was made of the murders. The arrest was kept low key and no announcement was made to the media that a suspected serial killer had been arrested. Their caution was well advised, for as yet the police had no murder weapon – and no Tyria Moore.

CHAPTER FOURTEEN

AILEEN WUORNOS'S CONFESSION – IN HER OWN WORDS

Tyria Moore was located on Thursday, 10 January by Major Dan Henry of Marion County Sheriff's Department. She had fled her parents' home and was living with her sister in Scranton, Pennsylvania. Once he had cleared any jurisdictional matters with the local police, Major Henry did something quite remarkable for a senior officer investigating a serial murder case. He booked into a local motel with one of his prime suspects, Tyria, and then he summoned Jerry Thompson of Citrus County and Bruce Munster of Marion County who flew to Scranton to interview her. In her possession were, among other things, a briefcase and clock radio identified as the property of Charles Humphreys, and other items the property of Curtis 'Corky' Reid.

In that motel room Tyria was informed of her rights but not charged with any offence or granted immunity. There was no plea-bargain deal either. Munster says he made sure she knew what perjury was, swore her in and sat back as she gave her statement. Within a short while she agreed to testify against Lee at trial, and she was involved with Munster, Henry and Binegar to sell her story for a television movie. Our three cops, having access to the entire investigation papers, would act as consultants.

Initially, Tyria told the police that she had 'sort of known' about the Mallory murder since Lee had arrived home with Richard Mallory's Cadillac. Lee had openly confessed that she had killed a man that day, but Tyria had advised Lee not to say anything else. 'I told her I don't want to hear about it,' she told the detectives. 'And then, any time she would come home after that and say certain things, telling me about where she got something, I'd say I don't want to hear it.' Tyria had her suspicions, she admitted, but wanted to know as little as possible about Lee's business. The more she knew, she reasoned, the more compelled she would feel to report Lee to the authorities. She did not want to do that. 'I was just scared,' she said, bursting into tears. 'She always said she'd never hurt me, but then you can't believe her, so I don't know what she would have done.'

The next day, Tyria accompanied Munster and Thompson on their return to Florida to assist in the investigation. A confession from Lee would make the case virtually airtight, and Munster and Thompson explained their plan to Tyria on the flight. Putting her under 24-hour surveillance, they would register her into a

Daytona motel and have her make contact with Lee in jail, explaining that she had received money from her mother and had returned to collect the rest of her things. Their conversations would be taped. She was to tell Lee that the authorities had been questioning her family and that she thought the Florida murders would be mistakenly pinned on her. Munster and Thompson hoped that, out of loyalty to Tyria, Lee would confess. Lee was aware, though, that the phone she was using was being monitored, and made efforts to speak of the crimes in code words, and to construct alibis.

The calls continued for three days. Tyria became even more insistent that the police were after her, and it became clear that Lee knew what was expected of her. She even voiced suspicion that Tyria was not alone, that someone was taping their conversations. But, as time passed, she became less careful about what she said. She would not let Tyria go down with her. 'Just go ahead and let them know what you need to know... what they want to know or anything,' she said, 'and I will cover for you, because you are innocent. I'm not going to let you go to jail. Listen, if I have to confess, I will.'

Over the three days, there were 11 conversations, some of which follow in abridged form:

Operator: *We have a call to Room 160 from Lee.*
Moore: *Uh, yes, go ahead.*
Wuornos: *Hey, Ty?*
Moore: *Yeah.*

Wuornos: *What are you doing?*

Moore: *Nothing. What the hell are you doing?*

Wuornos: *Nothing. I'm sitting here in jail.*

Moore: *Yeah, that's what I heard.*

Wuornos: *How... what are you doing down here?*

Moore: *I came down to see what the hell is happening.*

Wuornos: *Everything's copacetic. I'm in here for a... a... vi... uh... con... carrying a concealed weapon back in '86... and a traffic ticket.*

Moore: *Really?*

Wuornos: *Uh huh.*

Moore: *Because there's been officials up at my parents' house asking some questions.*

Wuornos: *Uh oh.*

Moore: *And I'm getting sacred.*

Wuornos: *Hmmm. Well, you know, I don't think there should be anything to worry about.*

Moore: *Well, I'm pretty damn worried.*

Wuornos: *I'm not going to let you get in trouble.*

Moore: *That's good.*

Wuornos: *But I tell you what. I would die for you.*

Moore: *Would you?*

Wuornos: *Yes, I would. That's the truth. I'll gladly die for you. And I'll just wait and see you on the other side. But you didn't do anything. Are you really by yourself?*

Moore: *Yes, I am.*

Wuornos: *Aw, I'm so proud you work in a factory...*

	What do you make?
Moore:	Buckets.
Wuornos:	Is it... is it boring?
Moore:	Time goes by pretty fast. Four dollars fifty-five.
Wuornos:	Oh, that's cool. Good. I'm so happy for you. When I get this cleared out, I can't wait to get out of here and get me another job and everything.
Moore:	I know.
Wuornos:	It is really mistaken identity. I'm telling you it is. I know it is. And I know it's one of those girls or somebody at work must have said, Hey, those look like... that looks like Lee and Ty and everything else, you know. God, Ty, I miss you so much... we couldn't pay the rent no more and everything. We had to go... that you had... it would... it was best for you to go back up and get... because I knew, I told you if you go up you'd find a job in a heartbeat... and I was thinking about going getting up there but I said, Shit, it's snowing and stuff and there's no sense in me going up there in the snow and everything when I didn't really have any real good, you know, help or anything like that.
Moore:	They're coming after me. I know they are.

Wuornos: *No, they're not. How do you know that?*

Moore: *They've got to. Why are they asking so many questions then?*

Wuornos: *Honey, listen... do what you got to do, OK?*

Moore: *I'm going to have to because I'm not going to jail for something that you did. This isn't fair. My family is a nervous wreck up there. My mom has been calling me all the time. She doesn't know what the hell is going on.*

Wuornos: *I... listen, you didn't do anything and I'm... I will definitely let them know that, OK?*

Moore: *You evidently don't love me any more. You don't trust me or anything. I mean, you're going to let me get in trouble for something I didn't do.*

Wuornos: *Tyria, I said, I'm not. Listen. Quit crying and listen.*

Moore: *I can't help it. I'm scared shitless.*

Wuornos: *I love you. I really do. I love you a lot.*

Moore: *I don't know whether I should keep on living or if I should...*

Wuornos: *I'm not going to let you go to jail. Listen, if I have to confess, I will.*

Moore: *Lee, why in hell did you do this?*

Wuornos: *I don't know. Listen, did you come down here to talk to some detectives?*

Moore: No. I came down here by myself. Just
           why in the hell did you do it?

Wuornos: Ty, listen to me. I don't know what to
           say, but all I can say is self-defence...
           Don't worry. They'll find out it was a
           solo person, and I'll just tell them that,
           OK?

Moore: OK.

Wuornos: And you'll be scot-free. You didn't do
           anything. All you did was work, eat and
           sleep. You never were around.

Moore: But, Lee, I knew for a year about the first
           one, at least. I mean, that's a hell of a
           long time.

Wuornos: I don't know. I think that you didn't
           know. I think I pretty much left you out
           of that.

Moore: No, you didn't. You came right out and
           told me about that one, and then I saw it
           on the news.

Wuornos: Ty, what do you want to do? Go to prison?
           Tell them everything. Although... it... I
           told you everything just before you left.
           You were thinking about turning me in.

Moore: When you did it the first time, I should
           have said something and...

Wuornos: Well, you were confused and scared, Ty.

Moore: I know I was.

Wuornos: You're not the one and I'm not going to

*let you go down on something you didn't
do. I love you too much to do that. I love
you more than... I love you right next to
God... You know what? I'm going to tell
you something.*

Moore: *What?*

Wuornos: *When I die, my spirit's going to follow
you and I'm going to keep you out of
trouble and shit and, if you get in an
accident, I'll save your life and everything
else. I'll be watching you. I probably
won't live long, but I don't care. Hey, by
the way, I'm going to go down in history.*

Moore: *What a way to go down in history.*

Wuornos: *No, I'm just saying... if I ever write a
book, I'm going to have... give you the
money. I don't know. I just... let me tell
you why I did it, all right?*

Moore: *Mmm.*

Wuornos: *Because I'm so... fucking in love with
you, that I was so worried about us not
having an apartment and shit, I was
scared that we were going to lose our
place, believing that we wouldn't be
together. I know it sounds crazy, but it's
the truth... I just hope you find
somebody that loves you as much as I
do. I don't want you to live alone all the
rest of your life. You're a good person.*

Moore: After you, I may live by myself for the
            rest of my life.

Wuornos: Ty, I don't want them messing with you.
            You go first and then I'll tell them. OK?
            I'd rather have you with your parents.
            Alrighty? I just wish... I never went...
            met Toni. Because Toni turned me into a
            lesbian... then I fucked up because I...
            see, when I have somebody I love them
            all the way and I love them with all my
            heart and all my soul and all my mind.
            And I'll do anything. I go nuts.

Moore: You turned me against everybody. I won't
            trust a person for the rest of my life.

Wuornos: I love you very much.

Moore: I know that.

Wuornos: Will you get over me?

Moore: Yeah... I don't think it'll be any problem
            at all.

Wuornos: OK. I'm sorry. I know this hurts. It is
            hurting you a lot. It hurts me because I
            don't have a family and I'm thinking
            about you. And you got a family. I
            know. I wish I had you so I could hold
            you and hug you and kiss you and tell
            you how much I'm sorry. Here is a
            kiss... OK, I'm going to eventually
            confess. What time do you check out?
            There's a tap on the phone.

Moore:	*Eleven... really?*
Wuornos:	*Yep.*
Moore:	*I didn't even hear it.*
Wuornos:	*I heard a little tick.*
Moore:	*Well, I'm getting ready to leave so, if you want to go ahead and get it over with, go for it.*

'I was sure it was being taped,' Lee said later. 'The way she was talking. I felt it. The way she was able to come back to Florida so quickly. She was staying in a motel for $50 a night. Where'd she get $50 a night? But she kept crying, "They're going to destroy me. I might as well kill myself. I need you to talk to the cops so they'll leave me alone." So I went and told the police that she had nothing to do with the crimes. But I also told them 37 times that it was in self-defence.'

Lee did have one friend at the Volusia County Branch Jail. Marjorie Bertolani was a jail officer who befriended Lee; in her depositions, she recalled the conversations she had with her.

'What did she inform you?'

'I told my corporal, you know, that Ms Wuornos wanted to speak to me. She looked really upset. So Corporal Cresta let me inside the block. When I got to the sally port she had gone to the telephone. She signalled for me to come in. I went over to a couple of other girls that were by a table. Ms Wuornos was on

the telephone. She was very upset...

'I was going to go ahead and leave again and Ms Wuornos got off the phone and signalled for me to come over to the table. And I sat down with her at the day-room table. She was sobbing. She was very, very upset. She asked me if I... she said she had done something terrible, and she wanted to get something off her chest. She asked me if I was a Christian. I told her, yes, I was.

'She proceeded to tell me that she had done some bad things. And she was one of the people that was wanted on these murders. And I just kind of... I really didn't know much about the case. I knew she was our mystery guest, you know. We just treat them like anybody else.

'She told me she had this lover named Tessie. She had nothing to do with the murders. And they had gotten drunk one night, and she had said something to this girl, and that she wanted to confess. And I asked her if she had an attorney. She said, "No." I said, "Well, I suggest you get yourself one." I told her, "You know, anything that you said to me I have to tell to my supervisors."

'She said, "Well, I wanted to get it off my chest," and she would speak to anybody, investigators, police, anybody. She said she wanted to go to heaven. She was afraid she wouldn't go to heaven. That's why she was telling me. That's why she wanted to confess to someone.'

'What shift were you working that day?'

'Eight to four shift.'

'This occurred at what time?'

'This was about ten o'clock.'

'In the morning?'

'Yes, sir.'

'Had she, to your knowledge, up to that point been pulled from her cell and taken to any other area of the jail?'

'You mean like to be questioned or something?'

'Yes.'

'No, not at all. Nobody bothered her at all.'

'Was she, to your knowledge, taken later that day?'

'Yes, she was.'

'The block that she was in, they have a telephone inside that area?'

'Yes, they do.'

'And they can make collect calls out of there?'

'Yes, sir. She was trying to get hold of this Tessie. I don't believe she got hold of her that day. She was really upset. I don't know who else she had called.'

'You're saying that she was visibly upset. Was she crying?'

'Yes, she was sobbing.'

'For longer than a brief moment?'

'For the whole time I was at the table she was. She asked me what I would do. I said, "I'd ask for forgiveness, you know. I'd forgive myself." Because she was really very, very upset. Of course, anybody

144

that upset we really watch for suicidal tendencies.'

'Her emotional state was enough to at least concern you?'

'Yes, it was. She told me she had killed six, not ten.'

'Where did the figure ten come from?'

'I had no idea, sir. She said, "I killed six, I did not kill ten."'

'Did you at any point in time during that contact with her – you're familiar with Miranda warnings...?'

'Yes, sir. I just told her that she had the right to counsel before she even, you know... after she had said... I said, "Well, you should have an attorney. You should be telling this to an attorney." She said she wanted to get it off her chest, and she would talk to anyone. She said, "I'll talk to investigators, I'll talk to detectives. I want to get it off my chest. I want to go to heaven." She kept crying.'

'Did she describe any conversations she may have had recently with this Tessie?'

'Only that she loved her very much, and that she was a Christian and goes to church a lot, and had nothing to do with it, and really hated to see her go through this; and "she'd probably never talk to me again". Her words.'

'In talking about this situation, wanting to talk to someone, based on what she is telling you, why did she seem to want to get this off her chest?'

'Because she said she was a Christian. She said she had really studied the Bible before. She wanted to go *to heaven. She was afraid she was not going to heaven. She said they were going to give her the electric chair.'*

'Did she mention anything about wanting to protect this Tessie?'

'No. She said she had nothing to do with it. She had told her about something in one of those episodes that she had had. She was drunk, in a drunken state, and she had confessed this. And Tessie really didn't know anything about it.'

'Did it seem important to her to want to make sure people knew that Tessie didn't have anything to do with it?'

'Not really. It was more like she wanted to go to heaven. She was more worried about that.'

Shortly after 10am on Wednesday, 16 January 1992, Lee met investigators Lawrence Horzepa of Volusia County and Bruce Munster of Marion County. Her interview was both video and audio recorded. Her love for Tyria was such that she had to clear her lover's name; if she did confess, maybe she would go to heaven.

Lee was appointed two Volusia County assistant public defenders, Raymond Cass and Donald Jacobsen, but it was in the presence of assistant public defender Michael O'Neill that she confessed to the murders of Richard Mallory, David Spears, Charles Carskaddon, Peter Siems, Troy Burress, Walter Gino Antonio and Charles Humphreys. For the moment, however, she would go it alone.

The two detectives knew they were on a knife edge with

this first interview. Even though Tyria was in a position to have been an accessory after the fact, she would not now face prosecution. However, the officers, from past experience, knew that the best-laid plans often fail. If Lee changed her mind in a pique, going public that Tyria was equally as responsible as she was, there would be a national uproar. But they had an ace up their sleeve. Unbeknown to Lee, they knew how desperately she loved Tyria Moore. She would die for her.

Nevertheless, the cops had to be on their best behaviour. They plied her with coffee and cigarettes, and gave her a warm jacket to wear in the chilly office. With such attention, linked to her need to protect her former lover, the only true love in her otherwise loveless life, and seemingly a desire to find favour with the Lord – a sentiment which she later spat upon – Lee's confession poured from her like a torrent.

Bruce Munster began the interrogation. Here are excerpts from the pertinent areas:

Munster: What I'm going to do is I'm going to preface the tape so that there isn't any doubt about anything that's going on. I'll be straight up front with you if you'll be straight up front with me, OK?

Wuornos: I would like to know if I wanted to... if I wanted to be straight up with one thing right here and now?

Munster: Sure.

Wuornos: *The reason I'm confessing is there's not another girl. There is no other girl. The girlfriend of mine is just a friend. She is working all the time and she... she worked at the Casa del Mar. She was always working. She was not involved with any of this... and the person that was murdered. She didn't know it was... until after the car was wrecked. See, she didn't know anything. She's really, really a good person, an honest person, a working person and she doesn't do anything wrong. She doesn't do drugs and all that stuff. She's a real decent person that works a lot. She was my... my... roommate.*

Horzepa: *OK, so then what you're telling us is you're voluntarily coming forward to talk to us now.*

Wuornos: *Yeah. To let you know that I'm the one that did the killings.*

Horzepa: *OK.*

Munster: *OK. Now, let me read you your rights, OK? You have the right to remain silent. The constitution requires that I so inform you of this right and you do not talk to me if you do not wish to do so. You do not have to answer any of my questions. Do you understand that?*

Wuornos: Yes.

Munster: If you want an attorney to be present at this time or any time hereafter you are entitled to such counsel. If you cannot afford to pay for counsel, we will furnish you with counsel if you so desire. Do you understand that?

Wuornos: What does counsel mean?

Munster: An attorney.

At this point Lee started to cry.

Wuornos: Well, what's an attorney going to do? I... I know what I did. I'm confessing what I did and go ahead and put the electric chair to me... I should never have done it. See, most of the times I was drunk as hell and I was a professional hooker and these guys would take my offer. I'd give them a little shit sometimes, you know, and so when they started getting rough with me, I went... I just opened up and fired at them. Then I thought to myself, Why are you giving me such hell for when I just... I'm just trying to make my money... and you're giving me a hassle.

At this point, the interview stopped while Lee regained her composure.

Wuornos: *I don't understand why I would have... what would an attorney do? Help me from keeping... getting the death penalty?*

Munster: *I don't know that.*

Wuornos: *I don't know. I don't know that either.*

Munster: *It's your decision, Lee, I can't make it for you.*

Wuornos: *If I did get the death penalty, do they stick you in a little room all the time?*

Munster: *I don't know. I don't know.*

Wuornos: *I'm a good person inside, but when I get drunk, I don't know what happens when somebody messes with me. When somebody hassles me, I mean, I'm like, don't fuck with me.*

Munster: *Yeah.*

Wuornos: *I mean anybody would be like that. And... in other words, really deep inside I was going to... when I was a little girl I always wanted to be a nun. And when I got older, I wanted to be a missionary, and I really got into... then I had some back problems. Then I fell in love with somebody and I had bad... when I love somebody, I love them all the way. But what I did, I don't understand why I did it. I just don't. I just know that they... they kind of gave me a hassle. When somebody gave me a hassle, I decided to whip out my gun and give it to them. Of course I didn't really want to kill them in my heart, but I knew I had to. Because I knew, if I left some witness, then they'd find out who I was and then I'd get caught. I have to tell. I have to tell the truth.*

When gently pressed further, Aileen started to open up while Munster and Horzepa wisely kept quiet. As any first-rate interrogator knows, they would have to listen to claptrap before they got to the most important issues at hand. Allow the suspect to waffle on and on before getting to the nub of the matter – a straight confession to multiple homicide.

Wuornos: *And I just... I wanted to tell it... All I... I want to confess. I don't want my girlfriend in trouble. She doesn't deserve to go to prison or anything because she doesn't know... she knows stuff of what I said in drunken spews, but she was not there. She did not know nothing and she did not... you know, she didn't... she couldn't believe me, I mean, if she... if she wanted to believe me, I'm sure she couldn't hardly believe me, is what I'm saying. And she loved me. And I loved*

*her. And she was like, I can't believe me,
is what I'm saying. And she loved me.
And I loved her. And she was like, I can't
believe you would do something like this.
So... I just want her to be very, very... I
am doing this because I don't want... I
love her very much and she's so sweet
and so kind and so innocent. She's just a
real sweet girl. You know, I don't want
her to get into trouble. Because she didn't
do anything. See, I was... she was at
work. Casa del Mar. While I was going
out and hooking. I would hitchhike. A
guy would pick me up and I'd ask if they
were interested in helping me out
because I'm trying to make rent money,
you know. And they'd say how much and
I'd say 30 for head, 35 straight, 40 for
half and half, 100 an hour. And they, you
know, then they'd say, well, I'll take this
or whatever and then, now... I'm telling
you, I've dealt with a hundred thousand
guys. But these guys are the only guys
who gave me a problem and they started
giving me a problem just... this year...
the year that went by. So, I at the time, I
was staying with some guy and I noticed
he had some guns and I ripped off his .22,
a nine-shot deal. And I carried that*

around while I was thumbing around – I
couldn't believe the cops never searched
me. I got... I got a message for the cops.
You see a hitchhiker? Search them. They
would never search me. And, uh, uh,
anyway, so when I'd get a hassle, if the
person would give me my money and I...
I wouldn't do nothing to them. But if the
person gave me my money and then
started hassling me, that's when I started
taking retaliation. But I was... she was at
work while I'd be in Ocala or Homosassa
or... or, shoot, sometimes Fort Myers. I'd
leave for sometimes a couple of days. It
didn't happen too often. But I would and
I'd come back with a wad of money. She
knew I was tricking, but she thought I
was doing it decently, honestly. And I'd
say I made a lot of money because I
was... been gone for a while. She didn't
know I killed somebody. See what I'm
saying? And then when she found out
that I did, she left. She took off and went
back home. I told her to go home. You've
got something to do. Just go and leave.
Get out of my life. Because I don't want
you involved. She didn't do anything.
Yeah, she said, yeah, and she started
hating me. I don't blame her. She said,

it's easy to hate you. It's easy to get over you. And I lost someone very dear in my life that I cared about. And I loved her with all my heart. I just wish I never would have done this shit. I wish I never would have got that gun. I wish to God I was never a hooker. And I just wish I never would have done what I did. I still have to say to myself, I still say that it was in self-defence. Because most of them either were going to start to beat me up or were going to screw me in the ass... and I'd... as I'd get away from them I'd run to the front of the car or jump over the seat or whatever, grab my gun and just start shooting. Which they would be out of the car. Most of them would be nude because they took their clothes off, see. And then they didn't, you know, didn't think about running back to the car or anything. I would start shooting out... from out of the car, shoot at them. Did they find any prints on the car that was, uh, the wrecked one?

Munster: *Yes.*

Wuornos: *Did they find that Tyria's prints and my prints were on it?*

Munster: *Yes.*

Wuornos: *OK. So that's why I'm confessing*

*because, see, she didn't know it was a car
by a victim. She just thought I had...
somebody loaned it to me. And we just
went around and driving around all the
time and drinking and driving. And then
I told her I was too drunk and I asked
her if she wanted to drive and then she
had a... she said OK, so she... we're
driving down the road and she was going
a little too fast and I told her to slow
down and she couldn't control the curve
and that's when we wrecked. Then I
went through the fence, got in the back
of the car after it was wrecked, went
through the fence, drove it down the road
while it was still smashed to hell. I had
blood all over my shoulder and shit and
then I told her, I said, 'Listen, I'm going
to tell you something.' She said, 'What?' I
said, 'We can't let the cops know
anything right now. This is a cop car. I
killed somebody, Ty.' She said, 'What!' I
said, 'I killed somebody.'*

The officers nodded their heads in sympathetic agreement.
Smiling warmly, Munster lit Lee another cigarette and
passed it into Lee's trembling fingers. Lee took a long draw
on the cigarette and sighed.

Wuornos: *Even if she knew – which Ty did – most*
of the times I would tell her shit off the
wall when I'm drunk. I think when I'm
drunk, I get crazy. And if I told her
something I told her like... OK, because
remember the guy with the red car...
carpet? [Charles Mallory]. That was
found under the red carpet on 90... uh,
US 1? That was me. OK, I told her, I
said, I came home and I said, 'I was
riding my bicycle and I stopped in the
woods and dropped it off and I found a
guy under a carpet.' And I told her that.
She said, 'What!' And I said I found a
guy underneath a carpet. Then later on,
when I was really drunk, and it's like
truth serum or something, I told her I
killed him. But I don't know if she could
believe it or not. But she was pretty
much like, 'No, you're kidding.' And I
was, 'Yeah, I did.' But then I don't...
can't say that I really said that I really
meant it because I don't remember
because I'd be drunk but I'd be telling
her stuff and she didn't... wouldn't want
to believe it, see. Uh... so, what I'm
saying is that, even though I might have
said something to her, she didn't really
know the truth. She's very innocent.

*Really. She's not... look at Casa del Mar.
Tyria Moore's her name, she worked there
all the damn time, all the time this stuff
was happening and when I... the last
person who got hurt, she was up in Ohio.
She is innocent. It was me. I can tell
you... blow by blow, as much as I can,
everything. I'm being as honest as I can.
And she's... I told her if anybody comes to
talk to you, just be as honest as you can
be. Tell them that I told you or anything,
because you are very innocent of this stuff
and I don't want you to get in trouble for
it because you didn't do anything. I may
have told you stuff when I was drunk and
everything else, but you didn't know if
you believed me or not because... And she
said, 'But I... I remember you taking a car
and we were moving our stuff.' I said, 'I
know, but remember when I told you I
was borrowing it?' She said, 'No, I don't
remember that.' I said, But... I... and...
but... I don't know. It's all I can say is I
know that she did... she... she's innocent.
That's what I am saying. She's not
partake... she did not partake in any of
this. And... if... only thing that she would
partake in anything, it would be
knowing... it would be my lips saying to*

her something and she didn't know if she could believe me or not, is what I'm saying. See, she was... she was very innocent.

Munster: *And I hope you won't lie to me. OK?*

Wuornos: *Oh, I'm telling you the truth all the way.*

Munster: *So we can... we can sit here... we can sit here and wait till your attorney comes. We don't need to talk about the case or anything till you all come to some decision.*

Wuornos: *I don't care. I mean... I'm... like I been saying, I don't... I don't mind talking... I want this all... I'm telling you from the bottom of my heart, I'm telling you the truth about everything. I mean I can't be any truthfuller. I'm telling you, with... God by my side, I'm telling you the truth. So, don't worry. I'm telling you the truth, honest. I just got... I mean... this isn't a joke... I didn't mean to giggle there. I'm... I'm being very honest. That's all I can say. I... the only reason I'm doing this is because... number one, I'm guilty, number two, my girlfriend is not. She doesn't... didn't know anything. She was never around at the time that I... hurt these people. She was at work. She'd work, eat, sleep, come home and that*

was it. She's a very good person. She
doesn't do drugs. She might drink a little
beer now and then, but that's it. And
she's a real sweet person and she doesn't
deserve to get harmed in this because she
didn't do anything. And that's another
reason I'm confessing. Because they were
looking for two women and I want to
straighten it out that she was with me
with the car, but she didn't know the car
belonged to somebody that was
murdered... until after the wreck. And I
told her, I said, 'Man, Ty, I've got to tell
you something.' You know, in my mind.
So I said, 'Ty,' you know, I said, 'get in
the bushes, man,' you know, because I
knew some cars were coming, and so she
got in the bushes and she... she said,
'What the... what the fuck is the deal?' I
said, 'I got to tell you something,' and I
said, 'I killed somebody.' She said,
'What!' I said, 'I killed somebody, man.
This car is somebody I killed.' 'You idiot!
What are you, crazy? Why did you do
that?' and all that stuff. So, anyway, I
told her we got to get out of here because
I don't want you to get into trouble, you
know, you... you... know you didn't do
anything and, yeah, yeah, yeah, for sure,

you know, and all this stuff. So I told her to hide in the bushes every time a car went by. So, finally we started walking down the road and then those paramedics were trying... came by the road with a fire truck I think. And then we told them that we were hitchhiking... two guys... I lied... I did all the talking. I said to two guys who picked us up and we got in a wreck and they... no, wait... no I didn't... I said two guys picked us up and they dropped us off and we're on our way to Daytona and they told us this is where, you know, you can get to Daytona... and this... but, it was the wrong road and all that stuff. And, uh, so then I told them, you know, we got to get going.

Horzepa: *The only way that we can begin to talk to you again about the cases is if you wish to voluntarily come to us and say, Look, I no longer want an attorney. I want to go ahead and talk about these things. But since you have invoked your right to the attorney...*

Wuornos: *Yeah, because maybe an attorney can help me because I know...*

Horzepa: *And we can't talk to you.*

Wuornos: *Yeah, because I know that it wasn't... I, in my heart, I know I self-defended*

Aileen swears the oath before her murder trial.

Richard Mallory, the video repair shop owner who was Aileen's first victim.

Peter Siems, a gentleman in every respect, was one of Wuornos's victims.

Courtroom drama. Aileen with her attorney, Billy Nolas (*above*) and, *below*, speaking to a detective.

Above: The Last Resort Bar in Port Orange, Florida, where Aileen was arrested.

Below: Tyria Moore. 'The only reason I hustled so hard all those years was to support her,' said Wuornos.

Above: Charlize Theron, who won an Oscar for her portrayal of Aileen Wuornos, with Dawn Botkins, a friend of Aileen's.

Below: The *Monster* première in New York. *From left to right*, Patty Jenkins who directed the film, Al Bulling, the owner of the Last Resort Bar and Charlize Theron.

The poster promoting *Monster*, the film about Wuornos's life.

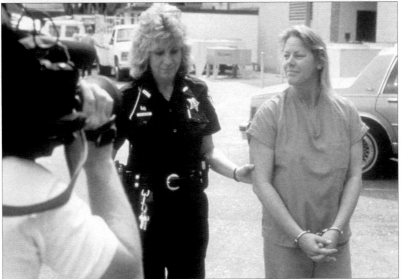

Above left: Charlize Theron with documentary-maker Nick Broomfield.

Above right: Protestors outside Florida State Prison on the day of Aileen's execution.

Below: The day Aileen Wuornos was adopted by Arlene Pralle.

myself so maybe I need an attorney.

Horzepa: OK.

Munster: *Did you contact one, Larry?*

Horzepa: Yes.

Munster: *One going to come down?*

Horzepa: Yes.

Wuornos: *Yeah, I know... I know that I have to defend myself because if I didn't, he probably would have hurt me, killed me, raped me or whatever. Beause I'm telling you, I'm serious. I have gone through at least 250,000 guys in my life at least. And never hurt any of them. Matter of fact, I became very good friends with them, you know, and they really liked me. And they always wanted to see me again and stuff, but I always gave them the wrong phone number because I didn't really want to be always having calls or I didn't have a phone anyway. So I'd give them the wrong number and stuff so... but, I mean it, I... what I'm trying to say is I never would have hurt anybody unless I had to, and I had to at the time. So yeah, I guess I need an attorney... you know I really suck.*

Munster and Horzepa were, they thought, on to a winning streak. They had manoeuvred themselves into the position of being the principal detectives when other officers were far better qualified to take the lead roles. This rankled with their colleagues who accused them of being 'office seats' and not good front-line investigators.

During her confession to Larry Horzepa and Bruce Munster, Lee returned again and again to two themes: she wanted to make it clear that Tyria Moore was not involved in any of the murders, and she was emphatic in her assertion that *nothing* was her fault, neither the murders nor the circumstances that had shaped her life as a criminal. She claimed that all the killings were acts of self-defence. Each victim had either assaulted, threatened or raped her. Her story seemed to evolve and take on a life of its own as she related it. When she thought she had said something that might be incriminating, she would back up and retell that part, revising the details to suit her own ends. Lee claimed to have been raped several times over the years and decided it was not going to happen again. In future, when a customer became aggressive, she killed out of fear.

Wuornos: *I'm very, very... I have to admit I'm scared about all this. I mean, I am very scared. I wouldn't have confessed if it wasn't for the fact that I don't want my girlfriend involved. I mean, I don't know, because I've thought about it many times, but I don't want her involved. Because she's not involved. I mean, you can ask*

*her questions and stuff but she didn't
know anything, she wasn't around and
I'm telling you, I love her very much to
the max, is what I'm trying to say. I love
her deep down inside very much. She's a
Chr– well, she's not a Christian but she
goes to... she used to go to a church and
she just worked, ate and slept and
watched videos at home, or watched TV,
Wheel of Fortune or Jeopardy or whatever,
and movies. She never did anything else.
Have... pop open a few beers because
she's not in... she's not guilty. And I'm
willing to take the punishment because
I'd rather confess that I did it so she
won't have to... I... in other words, she
doesn't deserve any punishment. She
didn't do anything. I don't know how to
express myself on this. I don't want you
to think I'm doing it because I love her
and am trying to protect her or
something, because I'm not. I'm doing it
because I love her and she's not guilty.
She didn't do anything. I'm being very
wide open and honest. It's a very
frightening thing for me to do... but I told
her I'm a bum. I don't... she was crying
her eyes out. My family's getting all
messed up. She... I didn't do anything.*

> 'You got me involved in all this jazz
> because of the car that you got wrecked.'
> Um... 'You need to go and tell them that
> you did it and get me straightened out on
> this.' And I said, 'Yes, Ty, OK, I will.' And
> that's why I'm doing this. Because I don't
> need her family or her getting messed up
> for something that I did. Hmmm. I know
> I'm going to miss her for the rest of my
> life. She's a real good person. So sweet
> and kind.

With Lee's attorney on his way to the jail, she could not resist another long, rambling dialogue which was intended to portray Tyria Moore as a saint:

Wuornos: *Oh, you guys, really... you can out me
under hypnosis, you can take a lie-
detector test, do whatever you can to
make me show you that Ty does not
know... did not do anything. Honestly. I
am being so honest, I can't be any
honester than I am. She... she's just a
good girl that met... got messed up with
a creep like me. I met her at Zodiac a
long time ago. Three years of good
friendship and being just... loving each
other and I screwed up the last year. I
asked her, I said, 'If I never done this*

would you have stayed with me?' And she said, 'Yes.' And so... I said, 'I guess you can... you can hate me now.' She said, 'Yes.' She said, 'It's not hard to do.' I said, 'Do you love me a little bit?' She said, 'I guess I do feel a little bit for you because, you know, I guess after three years you can still have a little love for me.' I said, 'But, yeah, I guess, go ahead and hate me because it'll be easier for me to get over you and you get over me.' But I don't have anybody, no family or nothing. She was my only friend in the whole world and that's why I loved her so much. But I loved because of her honesty. She never stole. My goodness, I got to tell you something. She was working at a Laundromat, and she found $125 in quarters in the back of the washer. She could have kept the money, but, no, she gives it to the people, gives it them back. And we were hard up for rent then. We needed rent money real bad. So I went out and made some money real quick. Then, I... when she was working as a manager at this Laundromat, I said, 'Ty, let me see 50 cents,' because there's quarters in the Laundromat, right? 'Ty, let me see 50 cents. I'm going go get a soda.' We lived three blocks from the place. She said, 'Hell, no.' She said, 'Go home and get the money. I'm not going to let you use any of this money.' Would you believe that they fired her, saying that she had taken some $600? But there was another guy who was working there and he died of cancer. And then there was another girl that was some kind of biker chick from Canada that would take over... uh... little... you know, for an hour or two... and I think they're the ones that stole the money. And she got fired for that and she did not take it, because, Honey, I... I mean, I mean... I'm thinking of her... and when I talk to her... I'd be with her all the time and we needed rent money, I had to go out and hustle for it. There's no way she took it. You see what I'm saying? She's a very honest person. I guess because we are lesbians, they'd always mess with us. She got fired at the Casa del Mar because we are lesbians. I know that's what the reason is. He's from Iran and, yeah, he didn't like the idea that he wouldn't... he couldn't get a piece of ass from her. Kept trying to get a piece of ass from all the girls at work. Yeah. He's the boss, you know. And so finally he said, 'Well, I knew it was coming to fire you.' And, she wouldn't give, you know, she's not going to... she's real sweet and innocent. She ain't going to. God, she's in love with me, you know what I'm saying? We didn't even have sex hardly. We had sex, I'd say, the first year, maybe three times and the next years, we didn't even have sex together. We were just friends. Just good friends. Hugging, kissing, but we were good friends. You know. So... that's why I'm saying... that's why I'm confessing because she's... shit, she wouldn't deserve anything because she didn't do anything, you know. I don't want her in trouble... for something that I honestly did. I know right now it's easy for me to confess. I know right now it's easy for me to say everything honestly now, when I get back to the cell I'll probably cry my eyes out. I'll go through a lot of hell, through court and everything else. I'll take a major toll in this. I understand. So, I know it's very frightening for me to confess. Because I know I'm probably looking at death, I'm possibly looking at life imprisonment. I don't know what I'm looking at, but I know one thing, I just

> *want to get right with God again and*
> *give this... I'll put my trust with the Lord*
> *and with the people here so everybody*
> *knows. I am so sorry... I mean I... I*
> *realise I don't have a family so I don't,*
> *sorry...*

Lee paused. Tears were now streaming down her face.

Wuornos: *I mean I... I realise I don't have a family*
so I don't understand. But when I... after
I'm... seeing Ty's family and everything...
I have never met the family but noticing
how Ty was on the phone and stuff, I
realise now how badly I used to hurt
some families. And the re– now... I...
these... these men were older men...
another thing after they were dead that
didn't bother me because I thought, Well,
they're older. They probably don't have
anybody hardly anyway so it didn't
worry me too much. But I didn't kill
them for that reason. I killed them
because they tried to do something to
me. But I think that, Well, they're old,
their father and mother's probably
deceased and so why worry about it and
stuff, I don't know. Creaky spots in my
head, I guess. [More sobs] I wish to

God... I wish I hadn't done it. Not that I'm feeling sorry for myself for what I'm going to play, I'm saying I wish I never had the gun, I wish I never, ever hooked and I wish I never would have met those guys. Because I wouldn't have had to do what I did if I hadn't been hooking, see. It's because of hustling, and the guy's going to physically harm me, that I have to harm him back. You see what I'm saying? Yeah. Beause if I wasn't hustling, if I wasn't hooking around, I would have never had a physical problem and I wouldn't have never had to hurt anybody. And I do have to say one thing, their families must realise that no matter how much they loved the people that died, no matter how much they love them, they were bad people because they were going to hurt me. So they have to realise the fact, that this person, no matter how much they loved them or how good they felt they were, this person was either going to physically beat me up, rape me or kill me. And I don't know which one. And I just turned around and did my fair play before I would get hurt, see? So, I would love to say to the families. I mean, that guy's going to...

*You stupid bitch. You killed my husband
or whatever, you know. Or my brother or
something. And I'd just have to say to
them, 'Listen, what are they going to do
to me...' I would be probably turning
around if I survived it, and say, 'You
stupid bastards. You almost killed me,
you almost raped me, you almost beat
the shit out of me.' So, you know, that's
how I have to look at it. I have to look at
it like that, too. So I can't really say that
they were sweet... You know, I know that
these guys... one guy had a weapon with
him. He had a .45 and I... it was dark
and he didn't know where he put it...
this is the weapon that I sold. And, uh, I
don't know where he put it. But I didn't
know he had a weapon, see, I had no
idea he had a weapon, but when he
started shitting on me that's when I
grabbed my gun and I started shooting.
And when I was done shooting him, and
I went through the car, and there was the
.45 sitting on top of the hood. I think he
was going to take the gun and blow my
brains out. So that's... another case. And
that's... I honestly have to say, if you're
hooking don't do it. I mean, I could help
people out so bad because I think I had...*

I have six chan– I had six times I almost
got killed. And I killed the person, see.
And I'm being very honest. Now, to
recollect all this stuff is going to be hard.
Because a lot of times I was drunk... and
after I'd done it, you know, I'd go and get
drunk so, wow, to remember everything
is going be a little bit difficult. I don't
even know their names. I can't even
remember their names.

After a break for coffee and cigarettes, Lee was introduced to Michael O'Neill, the attorney from the Volusia County Public Defender's Office. Now the police could continue in earnest. On numerous occasions O'Neill advised her to stop talking, finally asking in exasperation, 'Do you realise these guys are cops?' Lee answered, 'I know. And they want to hang me. And that's cool, because maybe, man, I deserve it. I just want to get this over with.'

Horzepa: *How many men have you actually shot*
and murdered? Shot and killed?
Wuornos: *Six. All I can remember.*
Horzepa: *Six... six men that you remember?*
Munster: *You forgot about the one [inaudible].*
That makes seven.
Wuornos: *No, because I only did six.*
Horzepa: *OK.*
Munster: *Well, we'll go over those six first.*

Wuornos:	Right. I think there's only six.
Horzepa:	OK.
Wuornos:	I know... I think it's six.
Horzepa:	OK, well... we'll go ahead now.
Wuornos:	OK, yeah, because... because if you showed me all the pictures of the guys, I can tell you, and if you show me a picture of a guy that... you know, if there's a seventh guy, I can tell you if I did or not because... I'm being very honest with you, as much as possible. I mean I am telling you the absolute, honest to God, so help me Lord, strike me with lightning in my heart right now, if I'm not telling you the truth.

Lee then went on to ramble for two minutes about how innocent Tyria was and what a sweet young innocent she had been while Lee had been out killing men. Then she was stopped short and asked when she aimed her shots.

| Wuornos: | I think I probably... it was... I always shot somebody, if I could, you know, as fast as I could, it would always hit right around this area. [She indicated to the centre of her chest.] Up here, right over... I always aimed to the mid-section so I know I shot them... usually it would be we both got naked and I was going to do |

an honest deed but I had a big fight.
They... they were either going to
physically fight me... either try to rape
me or something or they were going to
try to... you know, so they wouldn't have
to pay their... I don't know what they
were going to do. They just... started
getting radical on me and I had to... do
what I had to do.

Bruce Munster and Lawrence Horzepa had heard all of this soul-washing before from Lee. Now, with her lawyer present, they wanted to get down to business. The time for delicate niceties was over.

Munster: *OK, the guy with the .45 that you told*
me about before [Charles Carskaddon].
Now is he before this or after this, do you
remember?

Wuornos: *I think he was before. He was the second*
guy.

Munster: *Oh, the guy with the Cadillac was the*
second guy?

Wuornos: *No, the guy with the .45, I shot more*
than... over nine times. Because I was
pissed when I found the .45 on top of the
car. I reloaded the gun and I shot him
some more. And we were way out in the
boonies there and that's where he started

getting physical. He said, 'You fucking
bitch,' and I said, 'You fucking bastard,
you were going to blow my brains out,'
and I kept shooting him in the back seat
of the car. Then I drove over to 52 and
dumped the body.

Munster: *Was he still naked?*

Wuornos: *He was naked. I always stripped first.*
Mallory never stripped. He was just going
to physically fight me and get whatever
he wanted. I don't know without his
pants off, but it was his trip.

Lee went on to explain how Mallory picked her up.

Wuornos: *All right... he asked me if I wanted to*
smoke a joint and I said, 'Well, I don't
really smoke pot.' He said, 'You don't
mind if I smoke some?' I said, 'I don't
care what you do. Do whatever you feel
like doing... it doesn't bother me.' So,
he's smoking pot and we're going down
the road and he says, 'Do you want a
drink?' and he has, I don't know what it
was, it was tonic and some jazz. I don't
know what kind of liquor it was. So I
said, 'Sure, that sounds good to me.' So,
we're drinking and we're getting past
Orlando and we're getting pretty drunk

now. *And we're continually going down the road and I... we're getting drunk royal. Then I asked him if he wanted to help me make some money because I need some money for rent and everything. He was interested at the time. So we go out and we stop at this place on US 1, but we spend the whole night drinking and... you know, having fun for a little while.*

Horzepa: *What's 'having fun'?*

Wuornos: *Like... just talking. He's smoking pot and I'm drinking and we're talking. Then he said, 'OK, do you want to make your money now?' Around probably five in the morning maybe. And I said, 'OK.' You know, so he's pretty drunk and I'm pretty drunk.*

Horzepa: *Now, describe this area where you're at.*

Wuornos: *We're past I-95, maybe a half mile up the road. There was a little spot that went into the woods.*

Horzepa: *And, you're off... which road?*

Wuornos: *US 1.*

Horzepa: *US 1. OK. Describe to me the spot in the woods, if you can. Was it small, large? Do you remember anything about it?*

Wuornos: *Well, it was dark. We couldn't hardly see to get in.*

Horzepa: How d'you find it?

Wuornos: We kind of drove looking for this road to go in and we drove back around and we saw a road go in.

Horzepa: OK, so you were looking for a cut-off in the woods.

Wuornos: Right.

Horzepa: A spot in the woods that was...

Wuornos: Right.

Horzepa: Already a trail?

Wuornos: Right.

Horzepa: OK.

Wuornos: So we go into the woods... so he gives me the money and I start to disrobe. Now the guy's getting really... kind of starting... now he's going to start getting, you know, kissing on me and stuff and... anyway, he hasn't disrobed himself at all.

Horzepa: Do you know what he was wearing?

Wuornos: I think he was wearing jeans and some shirt.

Horzepa: Do you remember if it was long or short sleeves?

Wuornos: No, I don't remember at all.

Horzepa: OK.

Wuornos: OK, so, anyway, we're in the front seat. He's hugging and kissing on me and all this shit so then he starts, you know, pushing me down. And I said, 'Wait a minute,' you know, get cool. 'You don't have to get rough, you know. This is... let's have fun. This is for fun, you know.' And he's telling me, 'Well, baby, you know I've been waiting for this all night long,' and stuff like that.

Horzepa: Now where are you when this is occurring?

Wuornos: In the front seat of the car.

Horzepa: All right, and you're sitting where?

Wuornos: On the passenger side.

Horzepa: And, he is sitting... where?

Wuornos: In the driver's seat, going against me.

Horzepa: OK. He's behind the wheel of the car?

Wuornos: But he's coming toward me.

Horzepa: OK.

Wuornos: The doors are open. OK. So then he's getting really heavy, you know, on me, you know, and stuff, and I'm going like, now he's getting to where he just wants to just, you know. Unzipped his pants, not take his pants off or anything, just start having sex and stuff. And I said, 'Well, why don't you just disrobe or something,' you know? 'I mean, why do you have to have your clothes still on?' Then he started getting violent with me. So we're fighting a little bit and I had my purse right on the passenger floor.

Horzepa: *What kid of purse did you have?*

Wuornos: *A... a brown purse.*

Horzepa: *Is that the same purse that you...*

Wuornos: *Oh, no, wait. I didn't have my brown purse. No, it's not the one I had. I had a blue bag and it had a zip on the side. OK, and it was unzipped because I... I wanted to make sure if anything happened I... I could use my gun. Things are starting to happen where he was going to... I was thinking he was going to roll me, take my money back, beat me up, or whatever the heck he was going to do. So I jumped out of the car with my bag and I grabbed the gun and I said, 'Get out of the car.' And he said, 'What... what's going on?' and I said, 'You son of a bitch, I knew you were going to rape me.' And he said, 'No I wasn't, no I wasn't.' And I said, 'Oh, yes you were. You know you were going to try to rape me, man.' So, anyway, I told him to step away from the car. Oh, no, no, no, I didn't. All this and another thing, OK, I know what happ– OK, I took... I got... I jumped out of the car, yeah, he was starting to physically do stuff to me... aw, this is a different story. God. See it's so long ago.*

Horzepa: *It's all right. Take your time.*

Wuornos:	Yeah. OK, I jumped out of the car. I pulled my gun out when he started to physically do shit with me.
Horzepa:	Now, what type of gun did you have?
Wuornos:	Nine... .22 nine-shot, you know.
Horzepa:	Twenty-two long rifle?
Wuornos:	No, it's a gun, like about this big...
Horzepa:	OK. Why did you keep that gun with you?
Wuornos:	I was keeping it for protection.
Horzepa:	Where did you get the gun from?
Wuornos:	I stole it from a guy at a house.
Horzepa:	How long before?
Wuornos:	Oh, God, I don't know. I think it was...
Horzepa:	Months? Years?
Wuornos:	I don't know, man, it might have been about, a couple of months ago... I might have got the gun just then. I don't... I can't remember. Like... like two days before or something.
Horzepa:	OK. That's no problem.
Wuornos:	Because, I can't remember. It's such a long time. I did a lot of stuff in the time, you know.
Horzepa:	OK, so you're back there. You jump out of the car...
Wuornos:	I jumped out of the car because he was physically starting to abuse me. And I remember now. He didn't even give me

any money. This was another guy. This
guy, he said, 'Well, I'll give...' No, I said,
'Well, I always take my money first,' and
he said he wanted to see how the
merchandise fit.

Horzepa: *This is what Mr Mallory told you?*

Wuornos: *Yes.*

Horzepa: *OK.*

Wuornos: *So I said, 'Well, since I've been talking*
to you all night long, I think you seem
like a pretty nice guy, you know, so OK,
let's... let's go have fun. So I started to
lay down and he was going to, you
know, unzip his pants. And I said, 'Why
don't you take your clothes off?' My
God, you know, I said, 'Well, it hurt to
do that.' Then he got pissed, calling
me... He said, 'Fuck you, baby, I'm
going to screw you right here and now...'
Something like that.

Horzepa: *Now where are you?*

Wuornos: *I'm in the woods with this guy and the*
doors are open.

Horzepa: *OK.*

Wuornos: *I remember that. And I said, 'No, no,*
you're not going to just fuck me. You got
to pay me.' And he said, 'Oh, bullshit.'
And that's when he got pissed. Now, I'm
coming back to recollection. OK, so

> *that's when we started fighting and*
> *everything else and I jumped out. He*
> *grabbed my bag and I grabbed my bag*
> *and the arm busted and, when I got the*
> *bag again and I pulled it out of his hand,*
> *that's when I grabbed the pistol out. And*
> *when I grabbed the pistol out, I just shot*
> *him in the front seat.*

Referring to Richard Mallory later in the questioning, Lee changed the earlier version of her account and claimed: 'See, one guy, he was trying to screw me in the ass and stuff… he was going to try to a… anal screw. You know, anal screw or whatever you call it. So I started fighting with him and I got to my bag and I shot him. And then when I shot him the first time, he just backed away. And, I thought… I thought to myself, Well, hell, should I, you know, try to help this guy or should I just kill him. So, I didn't know what to do, so I figured, Well, if I help the guy and he lives, he's going to tell on me and I'm going to get it for attempted murder, all this jazz. And I thought, Well, the best thing to do is just keep shooting him. Then I get to the point that I thought, Well, I shot him. The stupid bastard would have killed me so I kept shooting. You know. In other words, I shot him and then I said to myself, Damn, you know, if I didn't… sh– shoot him, he would have shot me because he would have beat the shit out of me, maybe. I would have been unconscious. He would have found my gun going through my stuff, and shot me.

Because he probably would have gone to get it for trying to rape me, see? So I shot him and then I thought to myself, Well, Hell, I might as well just keep shooting him. Because I got to kill the guy because he's going to... he's going to... you know, go, and tell somebody if he lives, whatever. Then I thought to myself, Well, this dirty bastard deserves to die anyway because of what he was trying to do to me. So, those three things went in my mind for every guy that I shot...'

Munster: *Did you watch TV?*

Wuornos: *I watched TV all my life.*

Munster: *Did you watch to see if the police...*

Wuornos: *I watched TV all the time, but after the crimes, yes I did.*

Munster: *To see what the police were doing?*

Wuornos: *To see if they had found the bodies.*

Horzepa: *OK. From all the shootings that you have told us about, for the most part, you've always gotten the drop on these guys. You've been able to get your gun and point it at them.*

Wuornos: *Uh huh.*

Horzepa: *Right?*

Wuornos: *Right.*

Horzepa: *OK. At that particular time, you were in control. Why didn't you just run? Why didn't you...*

Wuornos: *Because I was always basically totally*

nude with my shoes off and everything
and I wasn't going to run through the
woods and briars and the...

Horzepa: *No, but still, like I say, you're in control.*
You got that gun. You could go ahead and
get dressed while you had, you know,
them do whatever you basically wanted.
Why did you go ahead and... shoot these
people?

Wuornos: *Because they physically fought with me*
and I was... well, I guess I was afraid,
because they were physically fighting with
me and I... what am I supposed to do, you
know, hold the gun there until I get
dressed and now I am going to walk out of
here? When the guy, you know, might...
you know, run me over with his truck or
might come back when I'm walking
through the woods or something... uh,
have a gun on him too or something. I
didn't know if they had a gun or not.

Horzepa: *So was it... was it your intent, during*
each of these times, to kill this person so
they couldn't come back at you later?

Wuornos: *Because I didn't know if they had a gun*
or anything. I... once I got my gun, I was
like, 'Hey, man, I've got to shoot you
because I think you're going to kill me,'
see?

Horzepa: *What about the ones who didn't have a gun, like Mr Mallory?*

Wuornos: *I didn't know they had... didn't have a gun.*

Horzepa: *OK. So you were taking no chances.*

Wuornos: *Right. I did not know... what... had... they... what was in their vehicle. See?*

Horzepa: *OK.*

Wuornos: *I didn't know if they had it under the seat, close by them. I didn't know if they were in arm's reach of another weapon or what. See?*

Horzepa: *What made you take property... a lot of property or a little property from some and not from others? Was there anything there that...*

Wuornos: *I guess it was.*

Horzepa: *Motivated you to...*

Wuornos: *I guess it was after, it was pure hatred. Yeah, I think afterward, it was like, You bastard, you would have hurt me and, uh, I'll take the stuff and get my money's worth because some of them didn't even hardly have any money. They were going to... they were... some of them didn't have any money. Like that guy, uh, the drug-dealer guy... he had 20 bucks and he was... he wasn't going to give me any more money. The one with the .45 on the hood [Carskaddon].*

Horzepa: *Mmm. Mmm. So you just started living off the items that they had? Is that what you were doing?*

Wuornos: *No, I think I took them just for the fact that, you bastards, you were going to hurt me, you were going to rape me, or whatever you were going to do. Well, I'll just, you know, keep these little items so I don't have to buy them or something. I don't know. I just...*

Horzepa: *It was like a final revenge?*

Wuornos: *Yeah. OK. That would... that would do. Mmm... mmm.*

Munster: *Lee, after you shot one time, I mean you could have left. You could have taken their stuff and [inaudible].*

Wuornos: *I didn't want to do that because I was afraid that, if I shot them one time and they survived, my... my face and all that, description of me, would be all over the place and the only way I could make money was to hustle. And I knew these guys would probably... would, you know, rat on me if they survived and all this stuff... and I would... I was hoping that I... after what I had to do, that I wouldn't have gotten caught for it because I figured that these guys*

185

deserved it. Because those guys were
going to either rape, kill... I don't know
what they were going to do to me. See
what I'm saying?

Horzepa: So you continued to kill these men to
cover up when you... when you shot
these men. Mallory was the first. Is that
correct?

Munster: OK. You continued... you had to go ahead
and kill these men so that they couldn't
testify against you and have it all back-
tracked? From body to body then?

Wuornos: Oh, no, I didn't even think of that either.
I... I shot them because it was like to me,
a self-defending thing because I felt that
if I didn't shoot them and I didn't kill
them, first of all, if they survived, my ass
would be getting in trouble for attempted
murder, so I'm up shit's creek on that one
anyway, and... and... and if I didn't and
if... and if I didn't kill them, you know,
of course, I mean I had to kill them... or
it's retaliation, too. It's like, you bastards.
You were going to... you were going to
hurt me.

Horzepa: So now I'm going to hurt you.

Wuornos: Yeah. Mmm... mmm.

Munster: Yeah, all... all of these guys that you
shot, they seem to be older guys. Over

the age of 40. What is that?

Wuornos: *Because all of the guys that I dealt with were that age. Every... every guy.*

Munster: *You were dead wood for the younger guys?*

Wuornos: *No. Every guy I dealt with on the road was anywhere from... let's see... 37 and up.*

Horzepa: *Was that your decision? I mean, like the...*

Wuornos: *Yeah. Because I...*

Horzepa: *Younger guy in his twenties would stop...*

Wuornos: *Yeah, because, see, I don't do drugs or anything and I wanted to deal with people who didn't do drugs. I was looking for clean and decent people. But, like I say, it just happened that the last... this following year, that I kept meeting guys that were turning out to be ugly guys... to me. That they were... fighting.*

For three hours, Lee talked and talked, then she talked some more, despite the continuing advice from her attorney who effectively spelled it out to his client that she was putting her head in a noose. Lee's mitigation was that she had been the wronged person. A simple hooker trying to earn a fast buck, her victims had used her, treated her badly or tried to have sex without payment. Her only remorse appeared to be directed towards Tyria, the lover she had failed. She shed not a tear for the incalculable suffering she had caused to her victims and their next of kin. She wanted to 'make it good with God' before she died; this would soon change as the months passed inexorably by during which Aileen Wuornos would metamorphose into the true monster that she really was. But, for now, with attentive, seemingly understanding police officers hanging on her every word, Lee continued to spill the beans.

Larry Horzepa now turned his attention to the property Lee had stolen from her dead victims.

Horzepa: Is there any property that you would have collected from these victims that may be stashed somewhere? You might have put it in the woods or behind an abandoned house or anything like that?

Wuornos: No. Uh uh. I just flung them out the window as I'm driving or... or stopped and threw them and stuff like that. I couldn't even tell you where because they were way out in the country somewhere where I didn't even know sometimes where I was.

Horzepa: There's something I forgot to ask you. There's another guy that's missing that we haven't found. A guy that worked for the Kennedy Space Center. A guy that worked for the Kennedy Space Center and there was a white Oldsmobile and the car was parked in Orange County off of Semoran and 436. The guy had glasses on and this would have been right around the HRS guy's car [Charles Humphreys].

Wuornos: Uh...

Munster: It was a white car and he was driving from Titusville to Atlanta... it was a white two-door car...

Wuornos: No, I don't recall anything like that.

Munster: Do you have a picture of him, Larry?

Wuornos: Yeah, yeah, if you got a picture of him...

Horzepa: What was the name on that?

Munster: Reid. Curtis Reid.

Wuornos: Curtis Reid. I don't know that one. I don't remember anybody like that.

Munster: He worked at the Kennedy Space Center and he had a Space Center emblem on his windshield of his rear window and someone scraped it off. He had a lot of money. He just cashed his pay cheque. You might have had...

Wuornos: I never got anybody that had a lot of money.

Munster: He might have had a thousand dollars, something like that.

Wuornos: Oh, I never got anything like that. Uh uh.

Horzepa: No, I have a flyer of the emblem. I don't

have that one.

Wuornos: *I don't recall anything like that because I never… I never got a lot of money on it. The only money I got, the most was that one that I didn't know was a missionary dude, was like $400 [Peter Siems].*

Having settled this matter, Bruce Munster started asking about the various alibis Lee had used.

Munster: *Who's Susan Blahovec?*

Wuornos: *Oh, well, that's another fake ID I had.*

Munster: *How'd you get that one?*

Wuornos: *Oh, Lord, let's see, how did I get… oh, this guy in the Keys had a birth certificate and he told me to use it for… because I had a suspended driver's licence and he told me I could use that ID. Oh… because… and I had… I think I had a… that forgery warrant was at that time, I think. I had that on me. And he told me I could use this ID, that it was his wife's ID, that she had never… he hated his wife, big time. And that I could… she's never been in trouble and that I could turn that birth certificate and licence, but you don't get into trouble with it, you know, just use it for driving and stuff, so I did.*

Munster: All right. I think that's...

Wuornos: How in the world did you find out about Susan Blahovec now?

Munster: Oh...

Wuornos: And did I put my name on a motel as that or something?

Munster: No. You got some tickets with it.

Wuornos: Oh, OK, I remember that. All right.

Munster: I know about the time in 1974, you were arrested under the name of Sandra Beatrice Kretch.

Wuornos: Yeah.

Munster: Your neighbour.

Wuornos: Yeah. I was... I was young and she was 33 or something and the judge couldn't... I spent ten days in jail for that one. She got away with having to go to jail on her damn ticket.

Munster: How far did you go in high school?

Wuornos: Tenth and a half grade.

Munster: Why'd you quit?

Wuornos: Because my mother died and my father wouldn't let me stay at home and I was living out on the street. I just want... to know that I hope to God, that you guys do understand that Ty is not involved with this. She doesn't know. She thought that I had these cars rented or... or borrowed them and all this jazz, and she *wasn't too... too aware of what I was doing. I mean, she didn't know... exactly what was happening. I mean I... when I'd get drunk I'd say shit from the top of my head just to try to be a bad ass, because I was drunk. And... but she didn't have anything to do with these murders. She didn't have anything to do with anything. She just worked, ate, slept, stayed at home, went to volleyball practice and was just a good gal... I've dealt with a hundred thousand guys. But these guys are the only guys that gave me a problem and they started giving me a problem just this year... the year that went by. So I, at the same time I was staying with some guy and I noticed that he had some guns and I ripped off his .22, a nine-shot deal... So when I'd get hassle, if the person gave me my money and then started hassling me, that's when I started taking retaliation... I just wish I never would have done this shit. And I just wish I never would have done what I did. I still have to say to myself, I still say that it was in self-defence... Really inside, right inside me, I'm a good person. But, when I get drunk, like I said, I'd be drinking with these guys and...*

and when they started messing with me,
I wouldn't tou– I would never hurt
nobody. But, if they messed with me,
then I would. I'd just... I have to say I
was... I'd get just as violent as they
would get on me... to try and protect
myself.

Munster: I know what I wanted to ask you. You
said that you put the gun and a
flashlight, some handcuffs into the water.

Wuornos: Oh, yeah.

Munster: Over by the bridge around Fairview. Now
you walked to the... on the bridge
there... were you in the middle or
towards one side or the other?

Wuornos: Oh, when you go over the bridge...

Munster: Uh, huh.

Wuornos: ... there's the other little bank there...

Munster: Uh, huh.

Wuornos: ... and it's right underneath the bridge
there.

Munster: OK.

Horzepa: Is it actually in the water or did you hide
it up underneath the bridge?

Wuornos: No, it's... it's in the water.

Munster: OK. You took the gun and threw it
underneath there?

Wuornos: Yes.

Munster: Now did you throw the handcuffs

someplace else?

Wuornos: No, I just dropped them along... they're
           straight down... yeah.

Munster: All right.

Horzepa: Could you see them when they hit... hit
           the bottom of the...

Wuornos: No, but I know it's waist deep... around
           there. Because some guy said he had
           cemented that part out there. And he had
           to get his net untangled from the crab
           trap and he told me it's about anywhere
           from here to there, in the water.

Horzepa: Lee, would you be willing, if we needed
           you to, uh, go out with us to try to locate
           that .22 that you threw into the water...
           if you can show us the exact location
           where you had tossed it? Would you be
           willing to do that for us, Lee?

Wuornos: I am willing to do anything. I want to
           just let you know I'm the only one
           involved in this deal... stuff... shit.

Horzepa: Also, too, uh, later on, would you be
           willing to talk to other investigators...

Wuornos: Oh, no problem.

Horzepa: ... if needed, from the other counties that
           have cases involved.

Wuornos: I want all this out in the open and I want
           them to know that there's not two girls.
           Ty is as innocent as can be. There was

> only one person. It was me, because I'm
> a hooker and I got involved with these
> guys because they were phys– and it was
> a physical situ– because I'm telling you
> now, I'm serious, every day when I was
> hitchhiking, I would meet anywhere from
> five to eight guys a day and make... now,
> but some would say no, and some would
> say yes.

Munster: Mmm... mmm.

Wuornos: And I would make money. But they
> wouldn't abuse me or nothing. I'd just do
> my thing and make my money, stick it in
> my wallet and go.

Munster: OK. That about wraps it up. All right,
> now, I'm going turn the tape off and it is
> 2.21 in the afternoon.

Wuornos: Can I ask you something?

Munster: You certainly can.

Wuornos: Do you mind if I keep these cigarettes
> because I don't have any cigarettes at all?

Horzepa: You are quite welcome to them and I'm
> glad you didn't ask to keep my jacket.

Wuornos: Oh, yeah, that was warm. Thank you.

Horzepa: Sure, no problem.

Wuornos: I'm very sorry...

After getting the most pressing, and somewhat self-serving, issues off her chest, a resilient Lee settled down to jail life, her mood alternating between abject depression and joviality. She had been allowed newspapers, and she avidly poured over the notoriety she was now receiving from the world's media. Her emotions, which had originally centred around Tyria, started to take a back seat. Religion and turning to God was way back in the past. She was becoming a celebrity – a person of some import and, for the first time in her life, she felt she had at least achieved something of value. If she could beat the rap – and she was sure she could convince everyone that she had only killed in self-defence – she could make a mint and buy a decent attorney and her way to freedom.

The true nature of Lee's psychopathic personality was about to be unleashed; not, this time, in a car with a vulnerable man at some lonely place, but in a more insidious way in the county jail, where she was observed by corrections officer Susan Hanson.

Two days after Lee's interviews with police, Susan Hanson was on duty and assigned to keep an eye on Lee. Although this inmate was not supposed to be treated any differently to the other prisoners, a certain mystique had built up around the so-called 'mystery guest' – everyone was curious and everybody wanted a piece of the action that was focused on Lee Wuornos.

As cocky as one would like, Lee saw Officer Hanson peering through the glass panel of her cell, and said, 'Listen to this. They say here [in the newspaper] "This woman is a killer who robs, not a robber who kills." That's... sure, I shot them, but it was self-defence.'

Later, in her deposition, Hanson recalled that Lee said that she had been raped many times, 'and I just got sick of it… If I didn't kill those guys, I would have been raped a total of 20 times maybe. Or killed. You never know. But I got them first… I figured that at least I was doing some good killing these guys. Because, if I didn't kill them, they would have hurt someone else.'

Officer Hanson in took every word, but said very little in return. Her instructions were to listen and document as much as she could remember as soon as it was possible to get to her notepad. 'I shouldn't be telling you any of this,' continued Lee, 'but get this. I had these two guys say they were cops, or at least they flashed their badges at me. They picked me up and wanted sex but didn't want to pay. Said if I didn't they'd turn me in. One grabbed my hair and pushed me towards his penis. We really started fighting then so I killed them. Afterwards I looked at their badges and one was a reservist cop or something [Walter Gino Antonio was a Brevard County reserve deputy] and the other worked for like the HRS [Charles Humphreys was a supervisor for the Florida Department of Health and Rehabilitative Services, referred to as the HRS.]

'I had lots of guys, maybe ten to twelve a day,' boasted Lee. 'I could have killed all of them, but I didn't want to. I'm really just a nice person. I'm describing a normal day to you here, but a killing day would be about the same. On a normal day we would just do it by the side of the road if they wanted oral sex, or behind a building or maybe just off the road in the woods if they wanted it all.

'On a killing day those guys always wanted to go way, way back in the woods. Now I know why they did it: they're going to hurt me... I figured if these guys lived, and I got fried for attempted murder, I thought, Fuck it, I might as well get fried for murder instead.'

In her deposition, Officer Hanson said, 'She was laughing a lot when she talked to me. When she would talk about, specifically, how she shot the guy, the one guy with the .45, she just stood there. She was very... sometimes she would laugh, sometimes she was calm in explaining this. Other times she would just get very excited. She was never sad in any way. Never once did she say, "I'm upset about this." She just said, "If I hadn't killed him, he'd kill other people."'

The jailhouse medic also witnessed Lee's cheerful mood when he stopped by to give her some medication to calm her nerves. 'I never really saw her down,' he said. 'She was always jovial and boasted of having done 250,000 men in the past nine years.'

'We kind of looked at her a little strange for that,' said Officer Hanson. 'The doctor just kind of walked away after that, and she sat down and began reading the papers again.'

News that the police had secured a female serial killer's confession soon leaked out to the public domain and an avalanche of book and movie deals poured in to detectives, to Lee and Tyria and to the victims' relatives. Lee seemed to think she would make millions of dollars from her story, not yet realising that Florida had a law against criminals profiting in such a manner. She commanded headlines in the local and national media. She felt famous, and continued to talk about the crimes with anyone who would listen, including Volusia County Jail employees. With each retelling, she refined her story a little further, seeking to cast herself in a better light each time.

On Monday, 28 January 1991, Lee Wuornos was indicted for the murder of Richard Mallory. The indictment read:

In that Aileen Carol Wuornos, a/k/a Susan Lynn Blahovec, a/k/a/ Lori Kristine Grody, a/k/a/ Cammie Marsh Greene, on or about the first day of December, 1989, within Volusia County, did then and there unlawfully, from a premeditated design to effect the death of one Richard Mallory, a human being, while engaged in the perpetration of or attempt to perpetuate robbery, did kill and murder Richard Mallory by shooting him with a firearm, to wit: a handgun.

Counts two and three charged her with armed robbery and possession of a firearm and, by late February, she had been charged with the murders of David Spears in Citrus County and Charles Humphreys and Troy Burress in Marion County.

Lee's attorneys engineered a plea bargain whereby she would plead guilty to six charges and receive six consecutive life terms. One state's attorney, however, thought she should receive the death penalty, so on Monday, 14 January 1992 she went to trial for the murder of Richard Mallory.

The evidence and testimony of witnesses were severely damaging. Dr Arthur Botting, the medical examiner who had carried out the autopsy on Mallory's body, stated that he had taken between 10 and 20 agonising minutes to die. Tyria testified that Lee had not seemed overly upset, nervous or drunk when she told her about the Mallory killing. Twelve men went on to the witness stand to testify to their encounters with Lee along Florida's highways and byways over the years.

Florida has a law known as the Williams Rule which allows evidence relating to other crimes to be admitted if it serves to show a pattern. Because of the Williams Rule, information regarding other killings alleged to have been committed by Lee was presented to the jury. Her claim of having killed in self-defence would have been a lot more believable had the jury only known of Mallory. Now, with the jury made aware of all the murders, self-defence seemed the least plausible explanation. After the excerpts from her videotaped confession were played, the self-defence claim simply looked ridiculous. Lee seemed not the least upset by the story she was telling. She made easy conversation with her interrogators and repeatedly told her attorney to be quiet. Her image on the screen allowed her to condemn herself out of her own mouth. 'I took a life ... I am willing to give up my life because I killed people ... I deserve to die,' she said.

Tricia Jenkins, one of Lee's public defenders, did not want her client to testify and told her so. But Lee overrode this advice, insisting on telling her story. By now, her account of Mallory's murder barely resembled the one she gave in her confession. Mallory had raped, sodomised and tortured her, she claimed.

On cross-examination, prosecutor John Tanner obliterated any shred of credibility she may have had. As he brought to light all her lies and inconsistencies, she became agitated and angry. Her attorneys repeatedly advised her not to answer questions, and she invoked her Fifth Amendment right against self-incrimination 25 times. She was the defence's only witness, and when she left the stand there was not much doubt about how her trial would end.

Judge Uriel 'Bunky' Blount Jr charged the jury on Monday, 27 January. They returned their verdict 91 minutes later. Pamela Mills, a schoolteacher, had been elected foreperson and she presented the verdict to the bailiff. He, in turn, handed it to the judge. The judge read it and passed it to the clerk who spoke the words that sealed Lee's fate. 'We, the jury, find Aileen Wuornos guilty of premeditated felony murder in the first degree,' she told an expectant assembly in the courtroom. As the jury filed out, their duty done, Lee exploded with rage, shouting, 'I'm innocent! I was raped! I hope you get raped! Scumbags of America!'

Her outburst was still fresh in the minds of jurors as the penalty phase of her trial began the next day. Expert witnesses for the defence testified that Lee was mentally ill, that she suffered from a borderline personality disorder and that her tumultuous upbringing had stunted and ruined her. Jenkins referred to her client as 'a damaged, primitive child' as she tearfully pleaded with the jury to spare Lee's life. But the jurors neither forgot nor forgave the woman they had come to know during the trial. With a unanimous verdict, they recommended that Judge Blount sentence her to die in the electric chair. He confirmed the sentence on Friday, 31 January, first quoting his duty from a printed text:

> *Aileen Carol Wuornos, being brought before the court by her attorneys William Miller, Tricia Jenkins and Billy Nolas, having been tried and found guilty of count one, first-degree premeditated murder and first-degree felony murder of Richard Mallory, a capital felony, and count two, armed robbery with a firearm ... hereby judged and found guilty of said offenses ... and the court having given the defendant an opportunity to be heard and to offer matters in mitigation of sentence ... It is the sentence of this court that you Aileen Carol Wuornos be delivered by the Sheriff of Volusia County to the proper officer of the Department of Corrections of the State of Florida and by him safely kept until by warrant of the Governor of the State of Florida, you, Aileen Wuornos, be electrocuted until you are dead.*
>
> *And may God have mercy on your corpse.*

A collective gasp arose from the courtroom, diminishing the solemnity of the occasion. The sense of shock was less to do with the judge's sentiment than his choice of words. May God have mercy on your corpse? Did Judge Blount really say that? Corpse? Members of the media stopped with pencils poised in mid-air. He had got it wrong. Surely he should have said, 'May God have mercy on your soul.' Could they quote him? they whispered among themselves.

Aileen Wuornos did not stand trial again. On Tuesday, 31 March 1992, she pleaded no contest to the murders of Dick Humphreys, Troy Burress and David Spears, saying that she wanted to 'get it right with God'. After a rambling statement to the court, she concluded, 'I wanted to confess to you that Richard Mallory did violently rape me as I've told you. But these others did not. [They] only began to start to.' She ended her monologue by turning to assistant state's attorney Ric Ridgeway, and hissing, 'I hope your wife and children get raped in the ass!'

On Friday, 15 May, Judge Thomas Sawaya handed her three more death sentences. She made an obscene gesture and muttered, 'Motherfucker.'

For a time, there was speculation that Wuornos might receive a new trial for the murder of Richard Mallory. New evidence uncovered by the defence – not presented to the jury at her trial – showed that Mallory had spent ten years in prison for sexual violence, and attorneys felt that jurors would have seen the case differently had they been aware of this. No new trial was forthcoming, though, and the State Supreme Court of Florida affirmed all six of her death sentences.

CHAPTER FIFTEEN

THE EXECUTION

THE FOOD AIN'T ALL BAD. WE'RE SERVED THREE
MEALS A DAY. AT 5AM, 10.30 TO 11AM, AND 4 TO
4.30PM. THEY COOK IT IN HERE. WE GET PLATES AND
SPOONS. NOTHING ELSE. I CAN TAKE A SHOWER
EVERY OTHER DAY, AND WE'RE COUNTED AT LEAST
ONCE AN HOUR. EVERYWHERE WE GO, WE WEAR
CUFFS EXCEPT IN THE SHOWER AND EXERCISE YARD
WHERE I CAN TALK TO MY CELL MATES. LATELY, I LIKE
TO BE BY MYSELF. APART FROM THAT, I AM ALWAYS
LOCKED UP IN MY ROOM. I CAN'T EVEN BE WITH
ANOTHER INMATE IN THE COMMON ROOM.

'People think this is all painless and stuff like that. It
ain't! Basically, they suffer a lot. They are sort of
paralysed but they can hear. They drown in their own
fluid and suffocate to death really. Yeah, we get

problems. Sometimes the guy doesn't want to get on to the table. But we have the largest guard in Texas here. He gets them on that table, no problem. They are strapped down in seconds. No problem. They go on that mean old table and get the goodnight juice whether they like it or not.'

ASSISTANT WARDEN IN CHARGE OF EXECUTIONS NEIL HODGES
TO THE AUTHOR, HUNTSVILLE PRISON, TEXAS, 1995

Aileen Carol Wuornos shared Death Row with several faces familiar to readers of true crime. The first of which springs to my mind is Judias 'Judy' Buenoano. Aged 45, and popularly known as the Black Widow, she had been on Death Row since 1985. Convicted of poisoning her husband, drowning her quadriplegic son by pushing him off a canoe and planting a bomb in her boyfriend's car, she had the distinction of being the first woman to die in Florida's electric chair on 30 March 1998.

Deirdre Hunt was sent to Death Row in 1990, and her sentence has since been commuted to life.

Andrea Hicks Jackson, sentenced to death for shooting a police officer in 1983, has also had her sentence reversed.

Virginia Gail Larzelere, aged 49, has recently been given the death penalty for murdering her husband at Edgewater, near Daytona Beach, on 8 March 1991.

Ana M. Cardona, aged 40, was sentenced to death for aggravated child abuse and the first-degree murder of her three-year-old son in Miami on 2 November 1992.

At the time of her execution, Aileen Wuornos was 46

years old but looked a decade older. The condemned woman, wearing an orange T-shirt and blue trousers, was five feet four inches in height and weighed 133 lbs. The characteristic strawberry-blonde hair described by witnesses framed her face, but her eyes were constantly bloodshot. Always looking washed-out, her once-attractive looks had been replaced with a face that life had not treated kindly. She still had the scar between the eyes and burn scars on her forehead. Her body was marked with a long cut along her lower left arm and a crude appendectomy scar across the middle of her abdomen.

The cell in which Lee was confined measured eight feet by ten. It was painted a dull-looking pink, and the ceiling was quite high, maybe 15 feet, which made the room seem larger and more airy than it really was. She had a black-and-white television placed above the stainless-steel toilet on a varnished brown shelf. The furniture consisted of a grey metal footlocker that doubled as a desk, but no table and only a single chair. There was also a dirty, lime-green cupboard at the foot of a metal bed which contained her clothes and personal possessions. Everything had to be locked away at bed-inspection time which could be any time between 9 and 11am. The only view she had of the outside world was a parking lot and a high fence festooned with glittering razor wire. There were no bars in her cell, but a metal door with a small hatch separated her from the rest of the cellblock. It cost the state of Florida $72.39 a day to keep Lee in her place of incarceration.

She spent the long, solitary hours reading books on

spiritual growth and writing lengthy letters to her now adopted mother Arlene Pralle. Lee's lifestyle was spartan and monotonous, and the days and the years rolled indistinguishably and uneventfully past her locked cell door. In the knowledge that 11.3 years is the average length of stay on Death Row prior to execution, Lee knew that, when her death came, it would be a painful end to a painful life.

Up until the botched execution of 'Tiny' Davis, Florida administered executions primarily by electric chair and only later by lethal injection. For this reason she was sentenced to die in 'Old Sparky'. This three-legged electric chair, constructed from oak by prison personnel, was installed at the Florida State Prison in Starke in 1999. The previous chair, dating back to 1923, was also made of oak after the Florida Legislature designated electrocution as the official mode of execution.

When that fateful day arrived, her head and body hair was to be shaved to provide better contact with the moistened copper electrodes attached to her body by the execution team. Sanitary towels would be forced into her vagina and rectum, and cotton wool pushed into her nostrils and ears to prevent the leakage of bodily fluids. In Florida, executioners are anonymous private citizens who are paid $150 per death. A four-second jolt of 2,000 volts is applied, followed by 1,000 volts for the next seven seconds and finally 200 volts for two minutes. Electrocution produces visibly destructive effects on the body, as the internal organs are burned. The prisoner usually leaps forward against the restraints when the switch is thrown. The body changes colour, swells and may even catch fire. The dying person may also lose control of the bladder and bowels, and vomit blood. Lee knew all this, but appeared unfazed. 'Death does not scare me. God will be beside me taking me up with him when I leave this shell, I am sure of it. I have been forgiven and am certainly sound in Jesus's name.'

But Lee would die by lethal injection.

Millions of us have been into hospital and recall the jab being given prior to an operation. This pre-med injection causes one to relax before another injection brings about unconsciousness around the count of ten. This is how the idea of sending a condemned inmate to perdition by a similar means came about. The drugs were certainly available, and they were cheap to use. And there was an extra bonus: the proposition of putting someone to death, in this clinical sort of way, necessitated clinical surroundings. Gone were the dread gallows, the ominous electric chair with all its wiring and leather helmet and death mask. Gone, too, was the evil-looking gas chamber with its sickly green walls, its rods, tubes and linkages.

There were benefits as well for the state authorities. The whole idea would appeal to the media and public alike, for execution could not possibly be made more merciful. A team of paramedics would attend to the inserting of a needle into the victim's right or left arm, and a doctor would be, as with all executions, in attendance to pronounce death.

On Sunday, 29 September 2002, Lee was woken in her cell at Broward and told to shower and dress for the drive north to her place of execution. This would be the last day the hot Florida sun would strike her face, and it would be for only a few moments at that. Heavily shackled, she shuffled into daylight and was assisted into a Florida Department of Corrections truck. Ironically her route would take her north, along I-95 towards the Florida Turnpike, west to Wildwood, then up I-75 to Gainesville. Leaving tourist Florida, with its Miami Beach hotels and Disneyworld and orange trees, far behind, she now entered a poor, rural landscape.

Nick Broomfield describes the journey. 'Stretch after stretch of flat, unrewarding scraggly pine trees and truck farms passed her by. Tiny post offices, well-attended Baptist churches – a good deal of praying and singing, often stomping and hollering, in the name of the Lord goes on in this part of Texas. They turned north-east along US 24, 30 miles then the road opened out on to a broad plain. To the right is the Union Correctional Institution, and then the Florida State Prison itself, just a rifle shot away across the New River in Bradford County. Interspersed between the prison cattle standing motionless along the roadside were inmate work gangs out with their uniformed guards, who cradled shotguns and wore sunglasses that coruscated in the afternoon light. It was a banal vision of purgatory, the sullen, shuffling convicts toiling under a heavy sun that glinted hard at them from their keepers' shielded eyes.'

What is now the Union Correctional Institution was

formerly the original Florida State Prison, and what is now known as Florida State Prison Main Unit was constructed with the death chamber in 1961. Florida State Prison Main Unit's title was transferred to the East Unit in 1973, and the old Florida State Prison became the Union Correctional Institution. Lee would spend two nights here before her appointment with death.

Lee was held in a special security cell. The three walls were painted a dirty cream; the barred front of her cage, with an additional mesh screen, looked on to the landing. Lit 24 hours a day, the cell had no table, just a stainless-steel toilet, a hand basin and a bunk covered with a light-green blanket and a grey pillow.

On Wednesday, 9 October 2002, as Lee sipped her last cup of coffee, she contemplated the end which she knew would be painful; what she didn't know was that she was going to be injected with a combination of three drugs which would burn terribly.

Sterling Ivey, a spokesman for the Florida Department of Corrections, told reporters, no doubt with tongue in cheek, that Lee was awake at 5.30am and was in a 'good mood' and 'ready for the sentence to be carried out'. Ivey said that Wuornos offered no resistance and was cooperative when she was strapped to the execution gurney outside the death chamber, and then wheeled into the room so the assembled witnesses could watch her die. When the lethal drugs began to flow into her, it was a quiet death. Other than her final statement, and two coughs, she made no sounds, said Ivey, who witnessed the execution. 'She just closed her eyes and her heart stopped beating.'

During her last days of life, Lee had requested no religious advisers, chaplain or a last meal, Ivey said. 'Lee Wuornos refused an offer to eat a barbecued-chicken dinner that was fed to the rest of the prison population,' Ivey reported.

An hour before the dread act, the witnesses started to arrive through the main prison gate to be escorted to the death chamber. They might have noticed the sheeting now draped over the steel gates hiding the hearse that was waiting to receive the body. After being given a shakedown to check for hidden weapons or concealed cameras, they were led to the viewing room, which is separated from the gurney by a window and closed curtains.

Around 30 minutes before Lee would take her last walk, she was given a pre-injection of 8cc 2% sodium pentothal. Waiting silently in an adjacent room was the cell-extraction team wearing protective clothing and armed with Mace gas to subdue her if she caused trouble.

Finally, Lee was invited to leave her cell. She agreed, and no guard touched her as she walked the few steps to the chamber door which was opening before her. Lee paused momentarily when she saw the gurney with its white padding and cover sheet. Two arm supports were pulled out and she saw the brown straps dangling loose with an officer by each one. There were tears in her eyes.

Lee was strapped down, and the paramedics inserted

two 16-gauge needles and catheters into her right and left arms and connected them, via tubes, to the executioner's equipment, which was hidden from view. The doctor also attached a cardiac monitor.

The curtains were drawn back and the warden asked her if she had any last words to say into the microphone above her head. She replied, 'I'd just like to say I'm sailing with the Rock and I'll be back like Independence Day with Jesus, June 6, like the movie, big mothership and all. I'll be back.'

Lee looked scared, as over the next ten seconds she was given an injection of sodium thiopentone (a rapidly acting anaesthetic). She felt a slight pressure and her arm started to ache. She felt light-headed. After a one-minute wait, this was followed by 15cc of normal saline to ease the passage of 50cc pancuronium bromide (a muscle relaxant to paralyse respiration and bring unconsciousness) over a ten-second time period.

Lee would have felt pressure in her chest, a suffocating feeling that caused her to gasp several times for air. She coughed twice as her lungs collapsed. She was dizzy and hyperventilating, her heart beating faster and faster as the whole sympathetic nervous system was activated. This is called stress syndrome, a common feature during the first stages of dying.

As the poison saturated her body, Lee entered the second stage of death. She was unable to breathe or move, but she could still see and hear. Paralysed, she was not able to swallow at this stage, which often gives rise to witnesses thinking that the inmate is already dead, when they are not. During this short period, the autonomic nervous system becomes dominated by the parasympathetic nervous system, or the sympathetic nervous system fails. Lee's eyes dilated and the hairs on her skin became erect.

Then she was hit with another 15cc of saline and finally a massive dose of potassium chloride. In large doses, injected intravenously, this drug burns and hurts horribly because it is a salt and instantly throws off the chemical balance of the blood with which it comes into contact. It makes all the muscles lock up in extreme contraction. However, it would not reach all of Lee's muscles: the moment it reached her heart, it would stop it dead.

There was a few minutes' wait and, at 9.47am, Lee was pronounced dead. The curtains were opened for the witnesses to view the deceased.

The ashes of Aileen Wuornos were scattered at a secret location in Fostoria, Tuscola County, Michigan.

CHAPTER SIXTEEN

THE MOVIE

> I BELIEVE SHE [TYRIA] IS INVOLVED WITH MILLIONS OF
> DOLLARS OF BOOKS AND MOVIES AND SHE DOESN'T
> WANT MY ACQUITTAL BECAUSE, IF I GET CONVICTED,
> SHE GETS THE MONEY AND SO DOES MR HORZEPA,
> MUNSTER AND A LOT OF YOU OTHER DETECTIVES
> AND POLICE OFFICERS THAT ARE INVOLVED IN THIS
> AND ALSO THAT SHE IS CONCERNED ABOUT HER
> FAMILY, SHE LOVES HER FAMILY... SHE'S ACTING LIKE
> SHE DOESN'T KNOW ANYTHING... I GOT 289 LIES IN
> HER DEPOSITION... WHY IS SHE LYING SO MUCH?
> SHE'S AFRAID TO TELL ANYTHING, SHE'S EVEN AFRAID
> TO SAY IT'S SELF-DEFENCE.

I hold the documentary-maker Nick Broomfield in very
high regard. He made his name with two critically
acclaimed films, one on the suicide of rock singer Kurt

Cobain, the other on the murders of rap stars Tupac Shakur and Biggie Smalls. Nick was drawn to the Wuornos story because of the level of 'demonisation' that was washing over her, and the headlong rush to wrap up the movie rights before she had been charged and before questions had been asked about how she could so casually turn into America's first female serial killer.

In a three-page feature for the *Sunday Express* magazine, 28 March 2004, Nick wrote, 'The police and lawyers were interested in money. The first phone call I made to her lawyer for an interview I was told, "Yes – for $25,000." I was astonished.'

The idea of a movie about Lee Wuornos was first mooted by Jacqueline Giroux, a beautiful, blonde Hollywood starlet. Jackie had begun her production company, the aptly named Twisted Productions, in Studio City in 1985. Her CV at the time showed that she had produced a handful of movies, some of which she had penned herself, and she was particularly interested in women's stories.

In due course, Jackie Giroux found herself in the position of being able to talk to Ray Cass, an attorney who was currently representing Lee. To his credit, Cass explained that he was ethically unable to help her; however, he did call Russell Armstrong who had represented Lee in 1981. Moving with some speed, Armstrong called Giroux who said that she wanted the rights to sell Lee's story.

Armstrong agreed to this offer, later stating somewhat

cynically that there was a German company interested in this production, but only if Lee got the death penalty. This, it appears, suited all three parties. So, ten days after Lee's arrest, Armstrong visited her in jail clutching the contract – Giroux called it a 'deal memo' – which required the signatures of Lee, Giroux and himself. It was a pretty loose contract: it offered no dates, no percentages, only a string of loosely strung promises hinging on money from investors who still had not become evident. Then the word got around.

Shortly after the signatures were in place, Armstrong received a blistering letter from the Florida attorney general, Robert A. Butterworth, who put the cat amongst the pigeons:

This office has been advised that your client, Ms Aileen Wuornos, has been arrested and charged with at least two murders and that you represent her in these cases. It has come to our attention that Ms Wuornos apparently has entered into a contract or contracts with a filmmaking enterprise to tell her story.

Please be advised that in the event Ms Wuornos is convicted of these felonies or any additional felonies, it would be the intention of the State of Florida to file a lien against all royalties, commissions or any other thing of value payable to her or her assigns from any literary, cinematic or other account of her life story or the crime for which she may be convicted.

The State of Florida hereby gives notice that it is

against public policy for someone to profit from her own crime and that this lien will be rigorously enforced pursuant to Section 944.512, Florida Statutes. You are further notified that any individual or corporation who holds monies or other items of value derived from any account of this story holds these assets in constructive trust for the State of Florida and will be held accountable to the State.

Cass and Giroux also received similar letters, while Armstrong went to the state's attorney and explained that he was only acting in a civil, not criminal, capacity, adding, 'I know nothing about the murders.'

Cass told reporters, 'I had nothing to do with any sort of contract because we're prohibited from doing anything like that. I tried to put as much distance between that and myself as I could.' But none of this impressed circuit judge Gayle Graziano who blasted Cass from the bench in a subsequent hearing. 'He should not have brought in another attorney. He should not have acted as broker for the attorney. There's the appearance of impropriety in that appearance of brokering.' With their wrists well and truly slapped, the attorneys and Jackie Giroux were stung. It seems nobody had spotted Section 944.512 of the Florida Statutes.

Arlene Pralle, the woman who was soon to become a bedrock friend and supporter of Lee, attempted to unravel the problems by writing to Judge Graziano and explaining that Jackie had spoken to her and reported that she had

MONSTER: MY TRUE STORY

been approached by Armstrong who said he had a deal she might be interested in. She flew to Daytona Beach and stayed there for seven days while Russell Armstrong and Raymond Cass tried to get visitation rights. When that failed, Cass reported back to her that the best he could do was set up a telephone interview, which was something far short of what Jackie Giroux had anticipated.

On 14 February, Arlene Pralle and a friend went to see Russell Armstrong who denied knowing anything about a book or a motion-picture project; he suggested that, if they wanted to visit Lee in prison, they had better speak to Raymond Cass. After they had pestered Cass for three weeks, he returned Arlene's call by saying that this responsibility fell to Armstrong.

Meanwhile, the police were beavering away in the background. While the legal bunfight was continuing between the attorneys and Judge Graziano, the police were now getting in on the act, with Robert Bradshaw, attorney for the sheriff's office, being appointed to deal with enquiries from the media industry. While he acknowledged that he held no sway over the defence team, or Lee herself, he was able to advise on any police contacts, and possibly on Tyria, who was a state witness.

On Tuesday, 29 January, the day after Lee was indicted for the murder of Richard Mallory, Bradshaw summoned Bruce Munster and Steve Binegar to a conference. By pure coincidence, perhaps, the following day Tyria phoned the easily accessible Bradshaw, claiming that Munster had just told her to make contact and that the detective had suggested that, if she, himself and Binegar pooled their information, they might sign a package deal.

As the days passed, Russell Armstrong told Lee that she was not entitled to a dime for the rights to her story. She felt cheated and effectively told Raymond Cass to sling his hook. With mud flying at him from several directions, he was 'delighted to leave'.

At a hearing on February 1991, Judge Gayle Graziano listened while Lee argued why she wanted to get rid of Cass. However, she failed to mention that, seconds before Armstrong gave her the bad news, she was gleefully boasting, 'I'm going to be a millionaire. I'm gonna be more famous than Deirdre Hunt.'

Addressing the judge, hypocritically complaining that her civil rights were being violated, Lee ranted, 'Cass was always talking about books and movies before and after I got indicted, it still kept ongoing and I don't even want to have anything to do with his associate [Armstrong], because to me they're a clan of people that are just interested in making money. They're not interested in my case. Everybody in jail really respects me, likes me. These people do not care about my case.'

Lee demanded that she be given a female attorney and Tricia Jenkins, public defender in Marion County, who was already assisting Lee against the murder charges there and in Citrus County, was assigned to handle her case in Volusia County as well.

PART FOUR

MAD OR BAD?

CHAPTER SEVENTEEN

DAMAGED BEYOND REPAIR

If there is one particular slice of the Wuornos story which is of value to society, it is her childhood. Lee's dysfunctional formative years are typical of most, if not all, serial killers' early days.

The structure and quality of family interaction is an important factor in a child's development, especially in the way he or she perceives family members. Their interaction with the child, and with each other, is crucial. The FBI states: 'For children growing up, the quality of their attachments to parents and to other members of the family is most important as to how these children, as adults, relate to and value other members of society. Essentially, these early life attachments (sometimes called bonding) translate into a map of how a child will perceive situations outside the family.'

Psychotherapist, neuropsychologist and neuroscientist

Dr R. Joseph is highly recognised as a creative, insightful and profound theorist and scientist. He is one of a handful of experts on both the brain *and* the mind. In his *The Right Brain and the Unconscious*, he says that the inner core of a person, their essential character, remains largely the same. Yet the effects of a poor upbringing make an indelible mark on the young character: 'What it was becomes the foundation for what it will be ... Just as the living tree retains its early core, within the core of each of us is the Child that we once were.'

Through considerable research, the FBI has shown that over 70 per cent of serial killers suffer extreme psychological and physical abuse as children. In my book *Talking with Serial Killers*, we see this played out again and again: most have lost a parent, or both parents, during their early days. Many are unwanted kids and are adopted, as were Kenneth Bianchi and Ted Bundy. Interestingly, in the context of Lee, all three lost their natural fathers around the time of birth. I could cite dozens more.

These youngsters may suffer the social stigma of being labelled 'bastards'. The more devastating effect of not being able to bond with their natural parents will wreak havoc with that all-important part of their lives as they struggle to develop into mentally healthy human beings; they will be seriously handicapped in not being able to match, on any level, the happiness and family security enjoyed by their peers.

Many, such as serial murderers Henry Lee Lucas and Ottis Toole, were sexually abused. Others, like Michael

Ross, were beaten by their parents. Some engage in early drinking sessions, find comfort in drug ingestion and are troublesome, disruptive pupils at school. A few become juvenile sadists. Arthur Shawcross, who also suffered from parental upheaval, held a grim fascination for torturing and killing small animals and birds. Most come to the attention of the welfare authorities at some time, and most parents of these children are advised to seek counselling for their offspring. Tragically, they rarely do.

More often than not, many of these youngsters grow up to harbour deep-seated grudges against either a male or a female in particular. 'The trauma they suffer festers away and becomes a fantasy for getting revenge,' says Ian Stephen, a forensic psychologist who works with the police and the prison service in Strathclyde. It could be the father or the mother, an aunt or an uncle, and they may well mirror this hatred in later life, their prey becoming the repository for their anger and their earlier mental and physical traumas. Simply put, it's payback time.

Society ignores these issues at its great peril, for in doing so we are breeding evil. But, many will say, there are lots of kids out there who suffer abuse. They don't all turn into serial killers, do they? That, I would agree, is a clear and concise observation. However, one only has to look at the escalating rates of serious juvenile crime, often linked to heavy drinking in today's society, to realise that parents and society are failing. Our prisons are full of young criminals. Many will graduate into very serious crime – and the murder rates are rocketing.

However, one could never find a more apt example of this phenomenon than by looking at Aileen Wuornos – an innocent child who turned into a monster. In a nutshell, she copped the lot.

There are always two sides to a story. Lee has given her own account, one which was strongly contested by her adoptive brother. But, for all of Lee's faults, we are unable to say that she was born evil, and she most certainly did not enter this world with a genetic flaw, or biochemical imbalance, although on her natural father's side there was certainly bad blood.

The young Diane Wuornos was living a troubled life. She had gone with Leo against the express wishes of her parents. Lauri Wuornos, with good reason, detested him and had banned him from the house. With one unwanted child in Keith, Diane gave birth to another unwanted child with Aileen.

A naïve, well-intentioned girl, abandoned by a wayward husband who was a sexual pervert, Diane did all she could for her two children with the meagre tools at her disposal, but Troy, the twelfth largest city in Michigan, had no time for the likes of Diane and her kids. A friend of Lee's, Michelle Shovan, would later say, 'Troy was a community out of control, unsupervised by any social-welfare agencies, and there was no school liaison between schools, parents, the police and welfare officers. Nothing seems to have changed much since.'

In this uncaring community, Diane was unable to find

work or get welfare. Faced with these circumstances, she felt she had only one option: to abandon her children and run away. During this formative period, Lee should have seen and felt her mother's emotions. The negative mirroring had started.

Diane knew that her parents, especially her disciplinarian father, would never agree to take on Keith and Lee, so she asked them to babysit and never returned. It was emotional blackmail if you will, for who else would take on the kiddies other than their grandparents? They did the honourable thing in adopting them. Lauri held down a secure job with a stable income; but two additional children was undoubtedly a financial strain on the family budget.

By the age of six, it was becoming apparent to the Wuornoses that Lee was a problem child. When she caused a fire that nearly burned the house down, Lauri reacted in the only way he knew how: he gave the child a thrashing, and thereafter the beatings never stopped.

Lee would have been confused and disappointed. Her innermost thoughts would have told her that the mother she had known, the person who had held and loved her for four years, had suddenly vanished. The home that she had known for four years had gone. She had been thrust into a new, unfriendly, strange environment. There were new faces staring down at her. She was no longer the centre of attention, and Lee would be subconsciously vying for the attention she craved when it was being shared amongst three other young people.

Lee would not, or could not, have understood why this

had happened to her. She was far too young to comprehend such matters. However, deep in her psyche, there was a void. Most psychiatrists will agree that to rip a child away from its mother after a bonding period of four years can cause levels of subconscious mental trauma we cannot even begin to calculate. To start with, this form of early upheaval breeds uncertainty and insecurity. When things go wrong, children often withdraw into a world of their own. They suffer from learning disabilities because they cannot focus on the tasks at hand, their thoughts being elsewhere. They find it difficult to mix freely with their own peer group, and appear as loners. In this isolated world their thoughts turn inward; they start to brood.

So many serial killers have suffered the same mental trauma as youngsters, and I cite Kenneth Bianchi as but one example. Born illegitimate, adopted by a neurotic woman whose husband was an inveterate gambler – his debtors were forever chasing him for money and threatening his life – the young Ken went through at least five schools, six different addresses and was of such concern to his teachers that they recommended him for psychiatric help on no fewer than four occasions. Frances, his adoptive mother, explained to me that Kenneth became a problem child, yet she absolutely failed to accept responsibility for her own shortcomings in not taking the advice offered by her young son's tutors.

Aileen Wuornos was definitely suffering from serious psychological problems at a very early age. As the FBI will confirm, at least 70 per cent of serial killers have faced similar childhood traumas. Many of these people found an interest in playing with fire. Adding up all of Lee's problems to date, she was on the road to disaster.

For those readers who have read my book *Talking with Serial Killers*, you will recall that the sexual sadist Michael Bruce Ross suffered from an identical form of physical and emotional abuse. Michael, who is now on Death Row in Connecticut, is the state's only ever convicted serial murderer. As a kid, he was ordered by his brutal father to choose the tree limb he would be beaten with from the yard woodpile. He soon learned that the thicker the branch, the less painful it was. We see exactly the same thing with Lee, who was similarly forced to cut willow branches. Do we not find this young girl being laid naked over a table and whipped with a leather belt which she had to clean after its use? That child, already a loner at school and amongst her friends in the neighbourhood, would arrive home a little late in the sure-fire knowledge that a sick punishment awaited her at the hand of a brutal man.

We also know that Lee was having full sex from around the age of nine. We cannot even start to think that she was some kind of 'slut' at that age, as so many observers feel content to believe. She would watch all the other boys and girls engaging in healthy childhood relationships while she was ignored. Again, lost in a world of her own, any attention from older boys was welcome, even if it was for all the wrong reasons. Being bribed with cigarettes – a smoke in exchange for sex – may have partially satisfied the young Lee's short-term needs for friendship and attention, but all of this was being built on shifting sands. Once the boys, including her own brother Keith, had had their fill, they would leave her alone once again. Her psychological problems became further enhanced by the fact that she was known as a slut, with the unwanted sobriquets of the Cigarette Pig and the Cigarette Bandit, all of which further alienated her from the few companions she had. In reality, Lee had already entered the seedy world of prostitution, being paid for sex in kind. Lauri Wuornos had much to answer for.

The study of many serial killers shows that, apart from being loners and having been physically and psychologically abused as children, they move into the early teens holding a deep-seated grudge against those who have hurt them the most.

Of some interest is the fact that these people, with a few exceptions, rarely hurt the abuser; instead they transfer and vent their frustrations and anger on others cast from a similar mould. Ted Bundy, for example, who never knew his natural father, had a disruptive childhood, and carried with him to the end of his days the social stigma of being illegitimate. As a young man, he was withdrawn and a loner, unable to find meaningful work or true love. When he found this love, the woman soon abandoned him and, although he didn't lay a finger on her, he went on to slaughter up to 50 other women as punishment. This transference of frustration and hatred can be seen in many cases: Dennis Nilsen, Kenneth Bianchi, Henry Lee Lucas,

Ottis Toole and Harvey Carignan are a few. Aileen Wuornos was to be no exception.

Aged 11, Lee's world completely collapsed when Lauri Wuornos told her in the heat of the moment that he and Britta were not her real parents, and they wanted rid of her for good. Her heart must have been shattered. This news turned her mind completely. She hated her grandfather with a passion that knew no bounds.

We know that Lee's teachers noted that something was seriously amiss with her for some time. Tutors of the young are, or at least should be, trained to flag up a child who has learning problems or poorly developing social skills. In Lee's case, the school recommended counselling for the 14-year-old girl, but the Wuornoses were not interested. Had the young Lee received counselling at this stage in her life, had the Wuornoses paid heed to their adopted daughter's tutors, there might have been a different outcome. But no help was forthcoming; instead, another shockwave hit home hard.

Lee learned, for the first time, the true identity of her natural father. He had been a sex pervert and rapist. Lauri Wuornos gloated when he told her that Leo Pittman had just hanged himself while serving a life sentence in a maximum-security mental institution.

Lee flipped, and sought the friendship of Mr Portlock, a man who lived in her neighbourhood. Now totally disowned by her adoptive parents, she gave birth in a home for single mothers. On her release, Lauri told her that if she came back he would kill her. The baby was adopted and the wheel that had become Lee's first 15 years on this planet had turned a full circle. Then Britta died and Lauri died of carbon monoxide poisoning in his garage. Lee says she found the body.

Out of the 13 'family-background characteristics' the FBI have found adversely affect a child's later behaviour, among their study group of serial killers, Aileen experienced 11 of them: alcohol abuse, drug abuse, psychiatric history, criminal history, sexual problems, physical abuse, psychological abuse, dominant father figure, negative relationship with her male caretaker figures, negative relationships with both her natural mother and her adoptive mother, and she had been treated unfairly. A staggering 85 per cent. By FBI calculations, that would have placed her at the top of their high-risk register. When one considers that even Henry Lee Lucas, one of the most notorious serial murderers in criminal history, had a score of 77 per cent, with Ted Bundy further down the high-risk register at a mere 38 per cent, Lee was not off to a good start.

Towards the end of her days, and teetering on the black abyss of insanity, Lee would change her story, saying that she had come from a 'clean and decent family'; her adoptive brother would have people believe that that is correct. However, there are too many witnesses who testified to the contrary, so there is no doubt that during her early years she was damaged beyond repair.

Lee's early years are documented within these pages. However, all of her accounts are embroidered versions of her life mixed with impenetrable fantasies. To say that she was a pathological liar right to the very end would be an understatement. I will be emphatic in saying that getting to the truth is, and always was, an impossible task, even for Lee herself. She, like scores of other murderers, has cried wolf and lied so many times, we would not recognise the truth if it stared us straight in the face. Indeed, even Lee, herself a sociopath, would no longer know the truth if she were alive today. Such is the nature of a psychopathic personality.

We must ask ourselves why Lee killed for the first time. She had been with scores of men before she shot Richard Mallory. The truth of the matter – again whitewashed and glossed over by most writers, the media, the trial judge, the prosecutor, police and for the convenience of justice – is that Mr Mallory was an extremely dangerous and perverted individual indeed. One would have to stretch coincidence a very long way in thinking that this played no part in him becoming her first victim. Lee had taken many rides during the day prior to meeting Mallory. She had all the money she needed in her purse to pay the deposit on a new apartment for her and Tyria. The simple truth is that Mallory met his nemesis.

Billy Nolas, Lee's attorney at her trial, tried to prepare the jury for the mitigating factors which the defence team planned to present, and he made a telling point. 'You have observed Lee's behaviour,' he said. 'Why is Lee the way she is … she did not simply fall out of the sky. There are things that she was born with and things that happened to her along the way ... a world which has made her what she is.'

Three other defence psychologists claimed, using phrases that would enliven any Stephen King novel, that the world of Lee Wuornos is a 'chilling place, a malevolent place, an angry, out-to-get-her place, a threatening place full of perceived terrors'. She perceived the world as having evil spirits, ghosts, things that are beyond our control. She distanced people by seeing them as angels or demons. And she functioned, they all agreed, on the level of a very small child.

Dr Elizabeth McMahon had performed the necessary neurological, psychological and intelligence tests on Lee. She examined her for a total of 22 hours. Dr McMahon testified that the structure of Lee's brain was normal, 'but it does not function properly, like sand in a gas tank ... the condition is chronic, static, doesn't change and interacts with other problems.'

Lee was a borderline personality, which is defined by eight classic symptoms. Dr McMahon claimed that Lee evidenced them all: a pattern of unstable and intense interpersonal relations; impulsiveness; unstable moods; inappropriate, intense anger; recurrent suicidal threats; marked and present identity disturbance; feelings of emptiness or boredom; frantic efforts to avoid real or imagined abandonment.

'This, combined with the dysfunctional background, produced an unhappy, discontented woman who cannot cope with the world. Lee is always in a state of living on the edge. There is a sense of danger, striving just to get her physical needs met,' said Dr McMahon. 'She has some sense that other people are doing it OK, but she's not ... Miss Wuornos is probably one of the most primitive people I've seen out of the institution. By that I mean that she functions at the level of a very basic... a small child. Always making an attempt at some sense of security, some sense of contentment.'

When cross-examined, however, Dr McMahon was forced to agree that Lee was sane, and that she knew the difference between right and wrong. Any chance of rehabilitation was remote, if not impossible.

The *Oxford English Dictionary* defines 'monster' as 'an inhumanely cruel or wicked person'. Aileen Wuornos certainly had a dysfunctional start in life, and we cannot blame her for that. However, she became hooked on murder for murder's sake. Aileen Wuornos chose her own fate. She knew that if she committed aggravated murder in Florida she could face the ultimate penalty. She decided to kill not once, not twice, but many times, and for this we are obliged to label her a monster.

Most of us have a conscience. Aileen Wuornos had a black void.

CHRONOLOGY OF DATES
AND EVENTS

29 February 1956 – born Aileen Carol Pittman

1960 – Lee's mother abandons her

18 March 1960 – Adopted by her grandparents Lauri and Britta Wuornos

January 1971 – Lee's baby boy adopted

1971 – Lee's natural father hangs himself in prison

7 July 1971 – Britta Wuornos dies

1974 – Jailed for the first time

January 1976 – Lauri Wuornos commits suicide

March 1976 – Lee marries Lewis Gratz Fell

16 July 1976 – Lee's brother Keith dies of cancer

July 1976 – Lee and her husband separate

19 July 1977 – Lee and Lewis divorce

4 August 1977 – Fined for assault and battery

1978 – Attempts suicide with a gun

1981 – Moves into a mobile home with a boyfriend

20 May 1981 – Lee robs store at gunpoint

4 May 1982 – Imprisoned for robbery

30 June 1983 – Released

January 1984 – Hitchhikes to Smyrna Beach, Florida

1 May 1984 – Arrested for passing forged cheques

1985 – First lesbian love affair with a girl called Toni

30 November 1985 – Suspect in the theft of a pistol and ammunition

4 January 1986 – Arrested and charged with auto theft

2 June 1986 – Arrested for threatening a man with a pistol and demanding money. Bailed

8 June 1986 – Ticketed for speeding

June 1986 – Meets Tyria Moore

November 1986 – Arrested for grand larceny

March 1987 – Lee and Tyria move into a trailer at Ormond-by-the-Sea

1 December 1989 – Richard Mallory murdered and, later, his car discovered

6 December 1989 – Lee pawns Richard Mallory's property

13 December 1989 – Richard Mallory's body found

19 May 1990 – David Spears murdered

20 May 1990 – David Spears's vehicle found

21/22 May 1990 – Charles Carskaddon murdered

1 June 1990 – Spears's body discovered

6 June 1990 – Charles Carskaddon's body found

7 June 1990 – Charles Carskaddon's vehicle found

7/8 June 1990 – Peter Siems murdered

4 July 1990 – Tyria and Lee crash Peter Siems's car

30 July 1990 – Troy Burress murdered

31 July 1990 – Burress's truck found

4 August 1990 – Troy Burress's body discovered

6 September 1990 – Curtis Reid murdered

11 September 1990 – Curtis Reid's car found

11 September 1990 – Charles Humphreys murdered

12 September 1990 – Humphreys's body discovered

19 September 1990 – Humphreys's car found

13/15 November 1990 – Tyria leaves Florida for Thanksgiving

16 November 1990 – Bobby Lee Copus picks up Lee and narrowly escapes with his life

17 November 1990 – Walter Gino Antonio murdered

18 November 1990 – Antonio's body found

23 November 1990 – Tyria returned to Lee in Florida. Lee gives Tyria Antonio's ring

24 November 1990 – Antonio's car discovered

2 December 1990 – Lee throws her murder weapon into Rose Bay promising Tyria that she will never kill again

3 December 1990 – Lee and Tyria part company for the last time. Tyria hands back the ring

7 December 1990 – Lee pawns Antonio's engagement ring

10 December 1990 – Lee leaves lodgings

8 January 1991 – Lee spotted by police

9 January 1991 – Arrested

10 January 1991 – Tyria located in Pennsylvania

11 January 1991 – Tyria relocated to Florida. For three days she speaks on the phone to Lee in jail

19 January 1991 – Lee presented with a movie contract while in the county jail

28 January 1991 – Indicted for the murder of Richard Mallory

29 January 1991 – Police try to thrash out a $2.5 million movie deal with Tyria

14 January 1992 – Lee sent for trial

27 January 1992 – Found guilty of the murder of Richard Mallory

31 January 1992 – Sentenced to death. Received at the Broward Correctional Institute, Death Row

31 March 1992 – Pleads 'no contest' to the murders of Humphreys, Burress and Spears

15 May 1992 – Given three more death sentences

9 October 2002 – Executed by lethal injection